The *Whirl* Story Bible

Presented to

_____

By

_____

Date

_____

The *Whirl* Story Bible

LIVELY BIBLE STORIES TO INSPIRE FAITH

Edited by Erin Gibbons

SPARK
HOUSE
FAMILY

Minneapolis

24 23 22 21 20 19 18 17 16 15   1 2 3 4 5 6 7 8
Hardcover ISBN: 978-1-5064-0000-6
E-book ISBN: 978-1-5064-0001-3

Illustrations: Matthew M. Keller
Cover and book design: Mighty Media

Editor: Erin Gibbons
Writers: Kevin Alton, Erin Gibbons, Melanie Heuiser Hill, Cheryl Mulberry,
   Justin Rimbo, Julia Seymour, Kathryn Watson
sparkhouse team: Debra Thorpe Hetherington, Dawn Rundman,
   Elizabeth Dingmann Schneider
Reviewers: Melissa Cooper, Marc Ostlie-Olson, Nurya Love Parish

Whirl™ is a registered trademark of sparkhouse.

Library of Congress Cataloging-in-Publication Data
The whirl story Bible : lively Bible stories to inspire faith / edited by Erin Gibbons ;
illustrations, Matthew M. Keller.
      pages cm
   Summary: "Contains illustrated retellings of one hundred common Bible stories"—
Provided by publisher.
   Audience: Ages 3-10.
   Audience: K to grade 3.
   ISBN 978-1-5064-0000-6 (alk. paper)
   1. Bible stories, English. I. Keller, Matthew M., illustrator. II. Gibbons, Erin, editor.
BS551.3.W45 2015
   220.95'05—dc23
                              2015010808

Printed on acid-free paper.

V23363; 9781506400006; AUG2015

Welcome to
The **Whirl** Story Bible

Experience God's living word through the beloved stories in *The Whirl Story Bible*. Every story is told in an engaging format that makes the Bible stories come to life.

- Read the lively story retelling on one page as kids follow the action in the pictures on the other page.

- Engaging questions embedded into each story help kids make connections to their own lives through their responses.

- Characters from the Whirl DVD series (*Whirl: Ada & Friends* and *Whirl: Leo & Friends*) appear with every story. Young readers will enjoy comments, explanations, and humor from twin siblings Ada and Otto and from Leo and Ruby.

Stories from the Old Testament

Creation 6
Adam and Eve 10
Noah's Ark 14
Abraham and Sarah 18
Sarah Laughs 22
Isaac and Rebekah 26
Jacob and Esau 30
Jacob Wrestles 34
Joseph and His Brothers 38
Joseph Interprets Dreams 42
Joseph Forgives His Brothers 46
Baby Moses 50
The Burning Bush 54
The Ten Plagues 58
The Red Sea 62
Manna and Quail 66
The Ten Commandments 70
The Battle of Jericho 74
Deborah 78
Ruth and Naomi 82
God Calls Samuel 86
David Is Chosen 90
David and Goliath 94

Kings David and Solomon 98
Elijah and Elisha 102
Queen Esther 106
The Lord Is My Shepherd 110
Isaiah's Message 114
God Calls Jeremiah 118
Daniel and the Lions 122
Jonah and the Big Fish 126
Malachi's Message 130

Stories from the New Testament

The Annunciation 134
Mary's Song 138
Jesus Is Born 142
Simeon and Anna 146
The Wise Men 150
Escape to Egypt 154
Young Jesus in the Temple 158
John the Baptist 162
Jesus Is Baptized 166
Jesus Calls the Disciples 170
The Beatitudes .174
Love Your Enemies 178
The Lord's Prayer 182
Don't Worry about Tomorrow 186
The Parable of the Sower 190

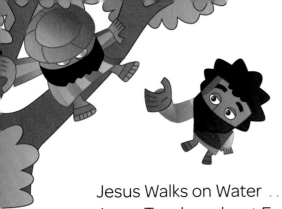

Jesus Walks on Water 194

Jesus Teaches about Forgiveness 198

The Parable of the Vineyard 202

Jesus and the Pharisees 206

The Greatest Commandment 210

Serving People, Serving Jesus 214

Healing at Simon's House 218

A Man through a Roof 222

Jesus Calms the Storm 226

Who's the Greatest? 230

Jesus Blesses the Children 234

A Camel through a Needle 238

Bartimaeus Sees 242

The Widow's Offering 246

The Transfiguration 250

The Good Samaritan 254

Mary and Martha 258

The Lost Sheep and Lost Coin 262

The Prodigal Son 266

Jesus Heals Ten 270

Zacchaeus 274

Water into Wine 278

Nicodemus 282

The Woman at the Well 286

Jesus Feeds 5,000 290
The Good Shepherd 294
Jesus Raises Lazarus 298
Mary Anoints Jesus 302
Jesus the Vine 306
Jesus Enters Jerusalem 310
The Last Supper .314
Jesus Is Betrayed 318
Jesus Is Crucified 322
Jesus Is Risen 326
On the Road to Emmaus 330
Thomas Wonders 334
The Great Commission 338
Jesus Ascends 342
The Holy Spirit at Pentecost 346
Early Believers Share 350
Saul's Conversion 354
Peter Raises Tabitha 358
Paul and Silas 362
Roman Believers 366
Jews and Gentiles Together 370
One Body, Many Parts 374
God's Family 378
Rejoice in the Lord 382
Timothy's Report to Paul 386
Timothy's Faith 390
Taming the Tongue 394
Alpha and Omega 398
New Heaven and New Earth 402

Creation

GENESIS 1:1–2:4a

In the beginning, nothing made sense. It was chaos!

The earth hadn't taken shape yet. Darkness was everywhere.

But God's Spirit was already there, always moving, moving, moving. God decided to set things in order.

God made light and saw that it was GOOD!

God named light *day* and darkness *night*.

How can light and dark exist at the same time?

I tried to find something in my room in the dark once. Sometimes you just have to turn on the lights.

God created the sky and separated the water from the land. Plants and trees popped out of the ground. God filled the sea with all kinds of fish. And God saw that it was GOOD.

The sun shone brightly during the day. The moon glowed gently at night. Birds burst into the sky. Bugs buzzed through the air. Worms crawled through the dirt. The fields and forests thundered under the feet of all God's animals. And God saw that it was GOOD.

? ?

What's your favorite part of God's creation?

God created people, male and female. "I have placed my image on you. I bless you," God said. "All of this creation is for YOU. Eat the plants. Tend to the animals. Care for creation. And grow and grow."

God looked over all creation. It was VERY GOOD! Finally, God rested.

I love everything God created, but why spiders?

Adam and Eve

GENESIS 2:15-17; 3:1-7

God scooped up dirt and molded it into a person. God took a DEEP breath and breathed life into the dirt. Adam's eyes popped open. God smiled at the very first person ever created.

Trees and flowers sprang up from the ground. "I've created this garden for you," God told Adam. "I need you to take care of it. But don't eat from the tree in the middle of the garden. It's the tree of knowledge of good and evil."

God formed the dirt into animals of all shapes. Adam named each one. "Turtle, sparrow, leopard!"

God did not want Adam to be lonely. So God took a rib from Adam and created a woman. Adam named her Eve.

Is this why we have aardvarks and duck-billed platypuses?

Maybe Adam was running out of animal names near the end.

Adam and Eve tended the garden together. They named even MORE animals. "Fish, cat, cow!"

But one day, the sneaky snake spoke to Eve.

"I know why God told you NOT to eat from the tree of knowledge," the snake taunted. "If you do, YOU will know what GOD knows about GOOD and EVIL, and you will be like God."

Eve sniffed the bright fruit. "How would it taste?" she wondered. "How would it feel to know about good and evil?" She plucked two fruits and gave one to Adam.

? ?

What do you wonder about?

Adam and Eve bit into the fruits. Immediately, they knew they had disobeyed. Ashamed, they covered their bodies with leaves and hid themselves from God.

I wonder what Adam thought when Eve handed him the fruit.

I wonder why they listened to a talking snake.

Noah's Ark

GENESIS 6—9

The world was a mess. ALL the people God had created were doing ALL kinds of wrong things—all except for ONE man named Noah. When God's people hurt each other, Noah helped them feel better. When they ignored God, Noah prayed.

"Noah," said God, "I'm going to flood the whole earth, but I will save you and your family. Build an ark. Fill it with two of every kind of animal."

Noah obeyed God and got to work. He measured and cut. He sanded and nailed. He filled the ark with two of EVERY kind of animal!

Rain clouds gathered in the sky. Noah's family hurried onto the ark with the animals. God shut the door. The rain began!

The ark must have been GIGANTIC to fit all those animals!

I hope God doesn't ask me to build anything that big. I only have access to cardboard and masking tape.

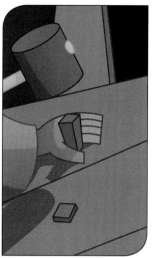

For 40 days and 40 nights it RAINED. Inside the ark, birds sang. Dogs barked. Snakes hissed.

? ?

What animal sounds can you make?

But one morning, everything was quiet. The rain STOPPED! Slowly, all the water dried up. Noah and his family jumped off the ark and wiggled their toes in the dirt.

Birds flew. Dogs ran. Snakes slithered. Every animal family came out of the ark.

Noah looked at the bright blue sky and saw a beautiful rainbow. Then God said, "This is my covenant to you and all people. I promise never to flood everything again. The rainbow is a sign of my promise."

Sometimes I get bored stuck inside on a rainy afternoon. What did they DO for 40 rainy days?

Abraham and Sarah

GENESIS 15:1-12, 17-18; 17:1-7, 15-16

Abram couldn't sleep. He tossed and turned, but he was STILL awake.

? ?
What do you do when you can't sleep?

Abram prayed:

"God, you promised that Sarai and I would have a baby.

"We're very OLD now.

"We STILL don't have a baby.

"Did you FORGET your covenant?

"Did you CHANGE your promise?"

God spoke to Abram. "Don't be afraid. I haven't forgotten my covenant. You WILL have a baby."

Abram was frustrated. "WHEN, God? How long do we have to wait?"

According to my calculations, Abram is right to be worried. At their age, it's very difficult to have children.

God told Abram, "Go outside." Abram rolled out of bed and rubbed his eyes. He walked outside.

"Look up. Count ALL the stars in the sky," God said.

Abram frowned. "God, no one can count the stars! There are too many!"

God's voice was gentle. "Abram, there are millions of stars in the sky. One day, millions of people will call you their father!"

Abram gulped. "Millions of children won't fit in my tent!"

God laughed. "It will be many generations of people. You won't see them all during your life.

"Abram, I'm giving you a new name," God continued. "From now on, your name is Abraham, which means 'father of many.' Sarai will be called Sarah. Someday, millions of people will call her their mother."

Abram trusted God. God would keep this covenant. God does not break promises!

Leo, you must be able to calculate how many stars there are.

Of course. The same number as there are descendants of Abraham!

Sarah Laughs

GENESIS 18:1-15; 21:1-7

Sarah looked at the wrinkles on her hands and touched Abraham's gray beard. They had waited MANY years, but still, NO baby!

"We're very old and have no child," Sarah told Abraham. "Did God forget about us?"

"God promised we would have a baby," said Abraham. "And God doesn't forget promises."

Sarah sighed. She thought maybe God had forgotten this time.

Abraham wiped his sweaty forehead. It was HOT! He squinted across the desert.

"Who are they?" Abraham wondered. Three strangers walked toward him. Abraham bowed to the three men and invited them to stay. "Please stay to rest and eat," Abraham told them.

? ?

Who do you invite to come to your home?

22

Wait. Abraham invited strangers to stay?

Yes, he welcomed travelers to his home.

"Sarah! Visitors are here," Abraham called. "Make some bread!" Abraham rushed to his herd so he could prepare meat and milk for them.

The visitors rested under a shady tree. Abraham gave them water to wash their feet.

Sarah shuffled around inside the tent. She mixed and patted and kneaded the bread dough. She listened to Abraham and the visitors.

"Where is your wife, Sarah?" one of the visitors asked.

"She's making bread to eat," said Abraham.

The three visitors smiled. "Soon she will be feeding a baby!"

"HA!" Sarah laughed. "I'm too old for babies!"

The visitors heard Sarah laughing. "Is anything too wonderful for the Lord?" they asked her.

Finally, God DID give Sarah and Abraham a baby! Just as the visitors said! Just as God promised! Sarah and Abraham named their son Isaac.

Do you know what Isaac's name means?

Ha-ha! It means LAUGHTER!

Isaac and Rebekah

GENESIS 24; 25:19-28

Abraham's servant traveled far. He stood by a well, tired and thirsty at the end of the day. His thirsty camels shuffled and kicked their feet. The servant waited. And waited. And waited.

"God, Abraham sent me to find a wife for Isaac," the servant prayed. "Show me who it should be. Have the right woman give water to me. And my camels too!"

Just then, a young woman came to fill her own jar with water. Abraham's servant jumped up. "Please, may I have a drink of water?" he asked.

"Yes, and I will give water to your camels too," she replied.

Abraham's servant clapped his hands. This was the one! This woman would be Isaac's wife! He ran up to her and took two big gulps of water. "What's your name?" he asked.

"Rebekah."

You can tell Rebekah's really great because she was kind to animals.

Rebekah agreed to become engaged to Isaac. Soon they were married!

? ?
Who do you know who's married?

Rebekah and Isaac wanted to have a baby. They waited. And waited. And waited.

Finally, God blessed Isaac and Rebekah with twin sons! The babies wrestled each other in Rebekah's belly.

Rebekah asked God why the babies were fighting. God told her, "One of your sons will be stronger than the other! The older will serve the younger."

Hairy Esau was born first. Smooth-skinned Jacob came second, grabbing his brother's heel! The brothers competed against each other from their very first day.

Hey, twins! Just like us.

That may be all we have in common with Jacob and Esau.

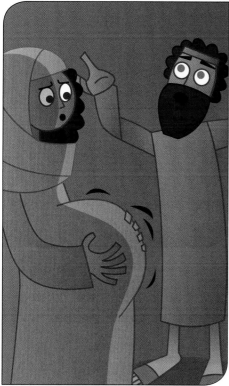

Jacob and Esau

GENESIS 27:1-40

Esau and Jacob were twin brothers. Very DIFFERENT twin brothers.

Esau grunted and flicked a flea from his hairy arm. He snorted and wiped his sweaty hands on his dirty robes. He went outside the tent to hunt.

Jacob wrinkled his nose. "My brother is loud and stinky and hairy," he thought. "I would rather stay inside." Jacob washed his smooth hands. He went to help cook with his mother, Rebekah.

"Jacob," Rebekah said, "come here." She told him her plan. "Your father is going to give Esau his one blessing. I want Isaac to bless YOU instead!"

Rebekah peeked into Isaac's room. He was snoring softly. Isaac was VERY old. He couldn't see well. Rebekah decided to TRICK Isaac into giving Jacob Esau's blessing. Jacob would pretend to be Esau!

? ?
What do you like to pretend?

Wait a minute . . . it sounds like Rebekah is playing favorites with her twins!

Mom would NEVER do that with us.

Jacob plugged his nose. Rebekah dressed him in one of Esau's stinky robes. Jacob closed his eyes. Rebekah wrapped his arms in animal furs.

"Go to your father," she said. "Tell him you are Esau."

Jacob stood by his father's bed. "Father," he said, "bless me."

"Come closer," Isaac croaked. Jacob stepped closer. Isaac sniffed. It SMELLED like Esau. He touched the furs on Jacob's arms. It FELT like Esau. He tried to see. It MUST be Esau!

Isaac blessed Jacob with a life full of FOOD and HEALTH and POWER.

Esau was FURIOUS with Jacob for stealing his blessing. Jacob ran away in fear.

Ada, I promise never to dress in stinky robes and pretend to be you.

Thanks, Otto.

Jacob Wrestles

GENESIS 32:22-31

All alone, Jacob stood watching his family get settled on the other side of the stream. He was surprised when he heard a THUNK! and felt a bump on his head. SMACK! He was knocked to the ground.

Jacob sprang to his feet and fought back. He grunted and pushed and pulled. He tumbled and rolled and kicked! He couldn't see WHO he was fighting. But he knew it was someone STRONG and POWERFUL!

"I can't lose," thought Jacob. Many years had passed since Jacob stole his brother Esau's blessing. He was FINALLY on his way home to face Esau. He couldn't stop now!

Jacob ducked and tackled and smacked. He wrestled with the mysterious man through the WHOLE night.

You would think after a few hours of wrestling a stranger, Jacob would have asked why they were wrestling.

The sun rose and light began to spread. The wrestling continued until . . . CRACK! The man knocked Jacob's hip out of its socket!

"OUCH!" Jacob yelped in pain. He grabbed onto the man.

"Let me GO!" the man shouted.

"NO!" yelled Jacob. He held on even tighter. "Not until you bless me!"

"What is your name?" the man asked.

"Jacob."

"I'm giving you a NEW name," the man said. "You aren't JACOB any longer. Your name is ISRAEL because you have struggled against humans and GOD. And you won!"

? ?

Have you ever heard of someone changing their name?

God blessed Jacob.

Jacob couldn't believe what had happened. He met GOD face-to-face!

A new name and a blessing! Jacob is a great wrestler and negotiator!

Joseph and His Brothers

GENESIS 37:1-28

Jacob had 12 sons, but he loved Joseph the most. When Jacob gave Joseph a new, colorful coat, Joseph showed it to his brothers. The brothers knew Joseph was Jacob's favorite and became jealous.

"Why does Joseph get a new coat and we don't?" they complained.

"I have an idea," growled Simeon. "Let's get RID of him!"

Joseph skipped along the path to see his brothers.

"Here comes the dreamer," grumbled Reuben.

Joseph's brothers GRABBED him and RIPPED off his colorful coat.

"STOP!" cried Joseph. "What are you doing?"

THUMP! Joseph landed in a deep pit. It was DARK and SCARY.

Eleven pairs of eyes glared down at him. Eleven voices laughed. Eleven brothers stomped away.

Joseph sat and thought. Why were his brothers so ANGRY?

What mean brothers! I would never tear off your coat, Ada.

I'm not wearing a coat, but thank you.

Joseph thought back to his dreams. In one dream, he was a bundle of wheat. His brothers were bundles, too, and they all bowed down to him. In another, he saw the sun, moon, and 11 stars bowing down to him. When he told his brothers about these dreams, they became ANGRY. The dreams meant that Joseph would be in charge of his whole family.

? ?
Who do you tell about your dreams?

"Our wheat and 11 stars bowed down to YOU?" they asked. "We will NEVER bow down to you, Joseph!"
Suddenly, Joseph was being lifted OUT of the pit.
"My brothers changed their minds!" thought Joseph.
Joseph's brothers DID change their minds. They decided to SELL Joseph to some traders passing by!
"That's it!" laughed the brothers. "Joseph is gone for good!"

I can't BELIEVE his brothers did that!

I wonder what will happen to Joseph next.

Joseph Interprets Dreams

GENESIS 39:20—41:57

Zzz . . . Pharaoh was sound asleep. Zzz . . . He dreamed of cows and grain.

? ?
What do you dream about?

The next morning, Pharaoh groaned, "I don't understand my dreams! Seven SKINNY cows swallowed seven FAT cows. Seven THIN ears of grain swallowed seven PLUMP ears!"

As Pharaoh's cupbearer listened, he remembered Joseph. When they were in prison together, Joseph listened to the cupbearer tell about his dreams.

"I dreamt I pressed three branches of grapes into Pharaoh's cup," the cupbearer told Joseph.

Joseph understood the dream. "In three days you will be freed from prison. Remember me when you see Pharaoh!"

NOW the cupbearer ran up to Pharaoh. "I know who can tell you what your dreams mean!"

Cows? Grain? Grapes? I usually dream about candy. Or race cars. Or candy race cars.

CLINK! The jailer unlocked the prison door.

TUG! Joseph was pulled out of prison, and he shaved his face, and changed his clothes.

PUSH! Joseph stood in front of Pharaoh.

Pharaoh told Joseph about his dreams: fat cows, skinny cows, plump grain, thin grain. "What does it MEAN?" he pleaded.

"God is telling you something important," Joseph said. "Egypt will have seven years of good harvest with LOTS of food. But then there will be seven bad years with almost NO food."

"That's AWFUL!" shouted Pharaoh. "What will we eat during the BAD years?"

"Store food during the good years. Eat it during the bad years," Joseph said.

Pharaoh was AMAZED at Joseph's words! He put Joseph in charge of storing food in Egypt.

So did the grain eat the grain?

Pharaoh was dreaming about the future, Otto. The grain actually means something else.

Joseph Forgives His Brothers

GENESIS 45:3-11, 15

Pharaoh made Joseph a governor in Egypt and put him in charge of preparing for famine. Joseph knew they needed to store food for seven years. Now Egypt was prepared for when no crops would grow.

Joseph's brothers in Canaan were starving. Their stomachs grumbled. No food anywhere! They traveled to Egypt to buy grain.

STEP, STEP, STEP. Joseph stood in front of his brothers. They bowed low to Joseph, the man in power. His own brothers didn't recognize him!

"Don't you know me?" asked Joseph.

"No, we don't," they said. They wondered why the governor would ask them this question.

"I'm JOSEPH! Your BROTHER! You SOLD me!" Joseph shouted.

"UH-OH!" thought Joseph's brothers. "We're in BIG trouble!" They turned to leave right away.

? ?
How do you feel when you're in trouble?

Joseph's brothers are in big trouble, all right. I bet Joseph gets even with them now!

Yeah. They were so mean to Joseph. There's no way he could forgive them, right?

"WAIT!" called Joseph. "Don't be afraid!"

The brothers stopped.

"YOU sold me, but GOD brought me to Egypt. GOD is in charge!"

Joseph's brothers couldn't believe what Joseph said.

"WHY would God do that?" Levi asked.

"Don't you see?" exclaimed Joseph. "God sent me to prepare for the famine!"

The brothers looked at each other. "Do you think it's true? Do you think he might forgive us?" they whispered.

Joseph stood closer to his brothers. Then he gave his brother Benjamin a BIG HUG!

"LOOK!" said the other brothers. "Joseph's NOT mad! GOD had a plan!"

All of the brothers hugged Joseph.

God's GOOD plan meant there would be PLENTY of food for all of Joseph's family!

 Well, that's a surprise. Joseph DID forgive them.

 I guess God CAN turn really bad things into really good things.

Baby Moses

EXODUS 2:1-10

"Hush, baby, hush," a mother sang as she rocked her tiny son.

The mother's face was worried. The new Pharaoh wanted to get rid of ALL the Hebrew baby boys. How could she protect her son?

Miriam, the baby's big sister, watched as their mother found a papyrus basket. "That's it!" said their mother. "I'll put him in this basket and float it in the river. THERE he'll be safe."

She walked to the river and tucked her son into the basket. Gently, she lowered the basket into the water. Sister Miriam crouched in the reeds to watch the basket float down the river.

A papyrus basket is not the ideal choice for a baby's boat.

They didn't have time to build a small ship, Leo. It was an emergency!

Splash, splash! Miriam heard women's voices. It was Pharaoh's daughter and her maids! Miriam held her breath. Would the princess see the basket?

YES! The princess peeked inside. Miriam's baby brother cried out.

"A Hebrew baby!" the princess exclaimed. She lifted him out of the basket. "Don't cry," she cooed.

Miriam's heart raced. She stood up and spoke to the princess. "I know someone who can care for your baby!" she shouted. Miriam raced home to get her mother.

The princess placed the baby in his mother's arms. He quieted. The princess smiled. "He likes you," the princess said. "I'll pay you to watch him."

The princess looked at the little baby. "I will name you Moses," she said, "because I lifted you 'out of the water.'"

? ?
Who named you?

Moses was safe, and his mother would see him every day!

Leave it to a princess to save the day! That's one of many things I have in common with princesses.

The Burning Bush

EXODUS 3:1-15

"FASTER!" Pharaoh's guards yelled. But the Hebrew people couldn't work any faster. They were HUNGRY. And TIRED. And HURT. They CRIED out, but Pharaoh still forced them to work.

Moses watched his people working. And hurting. He was sad and ANGRY. He felt there was nothing he could do to help them. He ran FAR away from Pharaoh.

Moses found work as a shepherd. One day while he was watching the sheep, something caught Moses' eye. What was THAT? A bush on FIRE! Moses stared at the bush. It was burning, but it didn't burn UP! Moses was curious. He stepped closer.

? ?
When have you seen a fire?

A voice came from the flames. "MOSES!"

Moses jumped. Did the bush speak his name? Cautiously, he answered, "Here I am."

That bush knew Moses' name! That's surprising!

It's a bush on fire that doesn't burn up and it can talk AND it knows Moses' name, and you think only one thing is surprising?

"Take off your sandals," the voice commanded. "This is holy ground."

Moses understood. The voice was GOD! He kicked off his sandals and bowed his face. Why would God talk to HIM?

God spoke. "I hear my people crying. They are HUNGRY. And TIRED. And HURT. Pharaoh forces them to work. I will take them AWAY from Pharaoh and make them free. Moses, you will tell Pharaoh to free my people."

Moses stammered, "Why would Pharaoh listen to ME? Why would your people follow ME?"

"Moses," God assured him, "I AM God. I will tell you what to say, and Pharaoh will listen. My people will be free."

Wait, so God is a bush?

No. God takes many different forms in the Bible to talk to people.

The Ten Plagues

EXODUS 7:14–12:32

Moses stood bravely in front of Pharaoh.
"God says, 'Let my people go!'"
But Pharaoh said, "I'm the only god in Egypt, so, NO!"

So God sent ten plagues to make Pharaoh listen.

ONE: The river changed from water to blood.
Nothing to DRINK!
Moses said, "Let them GO!" Pharaoh said, "NO!"

TWO: Slimy frogs hopped into town.
Frogs on every bed and table!
Moses said, "Let them GO!" Pharaoh said, "NO!"

THREE: Tiny gnats flew in a GIANT cloud.
Buzzing and biting!
Moses said, "Let them GO!" Pharaoh said, "NO!"

FOUR: Flies swarmed. Swatting didn't make them stop!
Moses said, "Let them GO!" Pharaoh said, "NO!"

? ?
When have bugs bothered you?

I wonder if Pharaoh knew what would happen.

FIVE: Animals got sick. Donkeys, camels, and sheep.
Moses said, "Let them GO!" Pharaoh said, "NO!"

SIX: Sores covered the Egyptians' skin.
Itchy, scratchy, OUCH!
Moses said, "Let them GO!" Pharaoh said, "NO!"

SEVEN: A big storm thundered.
Hail crushed the Egyptian crops.
Moses said, "Let them GO!" Pharaoh said, "NO!"

EIGHT: Locusts swept across the land.
Chewing and eating EVERYTHING green.
Moses said, "Let them GO!" Pharaoh said, "NO!"

NINE: God blocked the light of the sun.
Darkness all day and all night.
Moses said, "Let them GO!"
Pharaoh said, "NO! NO! NO!"

TEN: EVERY firstborn Egyptian child died.
The people shouted a loud cry.
Moses said, "Let them GO!"
Pharaoh cried and said, "YES! GO!"

More bugs and even darkness all day? It sure took Pharaoh a long time to finally say, "Yes."

I would have let them go as soon as there was nothing to eat.

The Red Sea

EXODUS 14:1-30

Pharaoh let the Hebrew people GO! They grabbed clothes, sandals, and bread. Then they RAN.

Wait! Pharaoh NEEDED servants and workers. His mind began to change as he watched them hurry away.

Pharaoh called his army together. He sent them to chase the Israelites across the desert.

The Israelites camped by the Red Sea. The rumbling of horses and chariots shook them awake. They panicked.

"Pharaoh's army is coming!"

"They're almost HERE!"

"We're TRAPPED!"

The Israelites turned and yelled at Moses. "We would have been safer as slaves in Egypt!"

? ?
What makes you feel safe?

"Don't be afraid," Moses assured them. "Watch what God will do."

I can't believe the Israelites wanted to go back to Egypt! Did they forget what it was like?

I can't believe Pharaoh changed his mind after telling them to go.

God told Moses to stretch out his hand, so Moses raised his arm. WHOOSH! A loud wind blew. God split the Red Sea down the middle!

The Israelites spotted DRY LAND in the middle of the SEA! They hurried across the sea on dry land. Walls of water towered over them.

But Pharaoh's army was right behind them! Just then, God sent a towering pillar of fire to confuse the soldiers. God clogged their chariot wheels. The Egyptians were STUCK!

The Israelites climbed out of the sea. Moses raised his hand. The waters crashed back down! Egyptian horses and riders were trapped in the sea!

What a great escape! Fire! Water! Chariots! It had everything!

That's because God knew how to get the people out of an impossible situation.

Manna and Quail

EXODUS 16:1-35

The feet of the Israelites were burning on the hot desert sand. They had been walking in the wilderness for months, but it felt like YEARS. There was no food, no water, and no end in sight.

The people complained to Moses.

"You should have left us in Egypt to die!"

"I'm so hungry!"

"Are you trying to starve us?"

God whispered a promise in Moses' ear. Moses listened closely. God told Moses that the people would have food—quail and manna. Moses trusted God. He got ready to talk to the people.

Quail and manna? Sounds delicious. I'm going to ask my chef to make some tonight!

Good luck. I have no idea what manna is.

Moses raised his arms and quieted the people. "God heard you complaining," Moses said to the exhausted Israelites.

"Uh-oh! Is God angry?" the Israelites wondered.

Suddenly, a huge cloud appeared! The voice of God, deep and clear, spoke to them.

"Tonight, you will eat meat," God announced. "And tomorrow, bread! You will KNOW that I AM God!"

? ?
What's your favorite food?

That night, a giant covey of quails strutted into camp. What a surprise! The Israelites filled their bellies with roasted quail.

The next morning, flaky manna covered the ground. They picked it up and tasted it.

"It tastes like bread!"

"It's salty!"

"And sweet!"

The Israelites collected baskets of manna. They had enough to eat each day. God sent manna so they were not hungry anymore!

 They ate the manna off the ground? Gross!

 I'm sure they brushed it off first.

The Ten Commandments

EXODUS 20:1-17

Mount Sinai was covered in thick black clouds. The clouds flashed with lightning and boomed with thunder. God wanted Moses to climb the mountain, so Moses started climbing.

Step by step, Moses climbed higher and higher. When he reached the very top, he stopped.

"MOSES!" God thundered. Moses looked up. A flash of lightning lit the sky.

"Tell my people I am the Lord your God. I rescued you from slavery in Egypt. I always come first. Do not make idols. Do not worship anyone but me!"

"Only use my name when you are talking about me. Choose one day each week to rest and worship me. Call this day the Sabbath."

God really knows how to get a person's attention.

God's voice thundered more. The ground shook under Moses' feet. Moses stood tall and still, listening closely to God's words.

? ?

When do you listen closely?

God wanted to help the people understand how to live as free people, loving God and caring for each other.

"Obey your mother and father," boomed God. "Don't hurt or kill anyone. Married people need to be faithful to each other. Always tell the truth."

"Don't take things that aren't yours. Be happy with what you have. Don't wish your neighbor's things belonged to you."

God gave Moses these commandments on two pieces of stone. Moses brought these stone tablets to the people.

Uh-oh. Do Mom and Dad know about all these rules?

Of course they do.

The Battle of Jericho

JOSHUA 6:1-20

Joshua looked up, up, up. He could barely see the top of Jericho's TALL city walls. He pushed on the city gates. LOCKED! The Israelites couldn't get inside.

"You will go inside Jericho, and I will be with you," the Lord assured Joshua. "Just DO what I SAY."

Joshua LISTENED to the Lord. Then he RACED to tell the Israelites what to do. "The Lord says to MARCH around the city walls," Joshua reported.

"For how long?" one soldier wondered.

"SIX days we have to march," Joshua answered. "The priests will blow rams' horn trumpets. The rest of the people will make NO noise. Not a peep, whisper, or sneeze! On the seventh day, we'll SURPRISE Jericho!"

? ?

When have you had to be very, very quiet?

No noise for six days? I could never do that.

I'd be surprised if you could make it for six minutes.

74

Joshua and the soldiers marched around the city for SIX days. The Israelite children tiptoed. They held their breath. They didn't want to make ANY noise.

On the seventh day, everyone woke up EARLY. They were ready to SURPRISE Jericho.

ALL God's people marched around the city SEVEN times. Then the priests blew their horns. Joshua yelled, "SHOUT! The Lord has given you Jericho!"

Girls shouted. Boys yelled. Dogs barked! Chickens squawked! The Israelites were LOUD!

CRASH! The walls of Jericho TUMBLED down! The people of Israel CHARGED into the city.

So what would have happened if they didn't follow the directions from the Lord?

I don't think the plan would have worked.

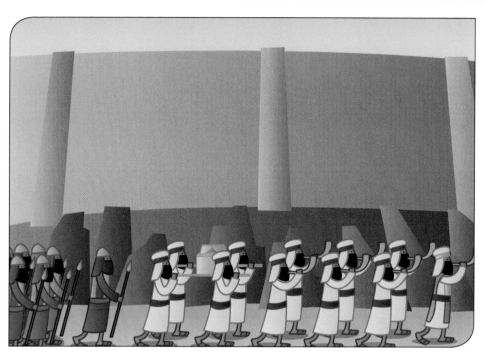

Deborah

JUDGES 4–5

Deborah was a judge in Israel. God chose judges such as Deborah to help and give advice to God's people, the Israelites. Most of God's judges were men, but not Deborah.

Deborah sat under a palm tree. She listened to problems. She gave answers from God.

"Sisera and his army are hurting and scaring my people," God told Deborah. "Get ready to fight. I'll help you defeat him!"

Deborah called a soldier named Barak. "Barak," Deborah began, "God says get ready to fight. Gather your soldiers. YOU will defeat Sisera."

Barak's eyes widened. "ME? Sisera has a HUGE army. He's very strong. I'm scared."

Deborah wasn't scared. "I'LL go with you. GOD will help us."

? ?

When have you been brave and done the right thing?

Barak is just one soldier, and the other side has a super-strong army. How is he going to lead the Israelites to victory?

Relax, Otto. Barak has Deborah on his side and they both have God.

Barak, Deborah, and TEN THOUSAND soldiers marched forward. Their STOMPING feet sounded like THUNDER. Their shields and swords flashed in the sun.

Clank! Clash! Thump! SMASH! They fought Sisera's army ALL DAY. Their arms and legs grew tired and heavy. But GOD made them strong. They kept fighting.

Barak's army WON the fight!

Sisera LOST. He sneaked away from the battlefield.

Deborah and Barak were so happy! They danced and sang: "The Lord heard our prayers. The Lord helped us win the fight. THANK YOU, Lord, for helping your people!"

So God will help me win if I pray first?

Do you think God likes fighting, Otto?

Well, probably not.

Ruth and Naomi

RUTH 1

"You don't need to follow me anymore," Naomi told Ruth and Orpah. "I have nothing left to offer you."

Many years earlier, Ruth and Orpah had married Naomi's two sons. But both sons died, so the two women now lived with Naomi, their mother-in-law.

"Go back to your parents' homes," Naomi said. "They can give you a place to sleep and food to eat. They'll take care of you." Ruth and Orpah sniffled and wiped their tears.

? ?
How does your family take care of you?

Orpah knew Naomi was a loving mother-in-law. But Naomi didn't have a home or work. Where would they sleep? What would they eat?

"I will always remember you," Orpah said. She gave Naomi a big hug. Then Orpah left. She traveled to her home country to live with family again.

But Ruth stayed with Naomi.

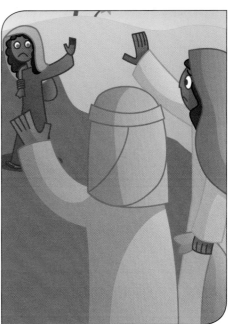

Wow, we're only a few sentences in, and this is already the saddest story!

I feel so bad for them all. Will things ever get better?

Naomi frowned at Ruth. "Why do you want to stay with me?" Naomi asked. "I'm going to Judah, where I was born."

Ruth grasped Naomi's wrinkled hand. Naomi shook her head.

"You don't know my country," Naomi continued. "You don't know the people there. You don't worship the same God we worship."

Ruth smiled and squeezed Naomi's hand. "I LOVE you, Naomi. Where you go, I'll go. Where you live, I'll live. YOUR people will be MY people. YOUR God will be MY God."

Naomi looked at Ruth's smile. She felt Ruth's warm hand. They were family!

Together, Ruth and Naomi walked the path to Judah.

In-law road trip!

God Calls Samuel

1 SAMUEL 3:1-20

When Samuel was a boy, he lived in the temple with a priest named Eli. Eli couldn't see, so sometimes he needed someone to help him day and night.

One night while Samuel was lying down, someone called his name: "Samuel!" He ran to Eli's room.

"Here I am!" Samuel shouted.

Eli jumped up from his sleep. "Samuel, I didn't call you. Lie down again." Samuel shuffled back to bed.

"SAMUEL!" he heard again. Samuel rushed to Eli a second time.

"Here I am!" he said, but Eli sent him away once more.

Samuel lived in the temple? That would be like living in our church.

Could we ring the bell or play the organ anytime we wanted?

"If ELI isn't calling me, who IS it?" Samuel wondered.

? ?

What sounds do you hear at night?

He heard the voice a third time. "SAMUEL! SAMUEL!" Again Samuel hurried to Eli's room.

"I didn't call you," Eli said, rubbing his tired eyes.

Samuel stomped his foot. "Someone IS calling me."

Eli realized it was the LORD! He told Samuel, "Next time, say, 'Speak, Lord, I'm listening!'"

A fourth time, Samuel heard his name. "Samuel!"

This time he whispered, "Speak, Lord, I'm listening."

The Lord said, "Samuel, I'm calling you. You will bring messages to my people. I will tell you what to say."

As Samuel grew, God gave him many messages to tell many people.

I wonder how Eli knew it was God talking.

Eli lived in the temple. He probably heard God talking all the time.

David Is Chosen

1 SAMUEL 16:1-13

Jesse's oldest son towered over Samuel. This son could lift a sheep with ONE hand. His legs looked like tree trunks. "This MUST be the king," Samuel thought.

God had sent Samuel to anoint the new king of Israel. But God surprised Samuel.

? ?
When has God surprised you?

"NO," instructed the Lord. "Not that one."

Jesse's second son stepped forward. He could throw a spear FARTHER than Samuel had ever seen.

"NOT that one," the Lord answered.

The third son puffed out his chest. He could wrestle his older brothers and WIN!

"NO, not him," the Lord said firmly to Samuel. "You're looking on the OUTSIDE. I'm looking on the INSIDE."

What does God see in a heart? Lots of blood?

No! God sees how you pray and what you think.

Samuel looked at four more sons. Four more times the Lord said, "No."

Then Samuel asked Jesse, "Have I met ALL of your sons?"

Jesse hesitated. "You want to see the YOUNGEST? He's out with the sheep."

"Please call him," Samuel requested.

"David!" Jesse called.

A red-cheeked little shepherd boy with bright, clear eyes rushed toward them. "Could THIS boy be the king?" Samuel wondered.

"YES," breathed God, "this is the ONE. He will be the next KING over Israel."

Samuel cleared his throat. "The Lord chooses DAVID."

David's brothers all spoke at once. "Little David? A king? I don't believe it!"

Samuel prayed. He anointed David's head with oil. The Lord would make David into a GREAT king.

If God says David will be a great king, I believe it. God's usually right about stuff like that.

David and Goliath

1 SAMUEL 17:1-49

Goliath was huge and strong and mean. He was a GIANT. A soldier. A Philistine.

David was clever and quick and small. He was a KID. A shepherd. An Israelite.

"COME and GET me!" Goliath roared.

Goliath's tiny eyes peeked out from his HUGE metal helmet. Shiny armor covered his chest, arms, legs, feet, and toes. The armor clanked as Goliath paced.

The Israelites ducked behind their shields. They were TERRIFIED of Goliath and the Philistine army. But David wasn't!

"What's wrong with everyone?" David said. "I'll fight this giant."

"NO WAY!" shouted King Saul, the leader of the army. "You're just a KID!"

David sounds so brave!

Mom would never let me fight a giant, or anyone else for that matter.

"I may be a kid," said David, "but God is with me wherever I go. And NOTHING is impossible for God!"

? ?
When have you been told NO because you're a kid?

King Saul and his soldiers shook their heads.
"Goliath is HUGE—you're SMALL."
"He has WEAPONS—you only have a SLING!"
"He's dressed for WAR—you're dressed for SHEPHERDING."
David, the Israelite shepherd, shrugged and took off running toward Goliath, the giant Philistine.
"What is that little BOY doing?" Goliath grumbled.
David spun his slingshot overhead. "You come at us with ARMOR and a SWORD," yelled David, "but I come at you in the name of the LORD!"
David chose a smooth stone for his slingshot and hurled it.
The stone whistled through the air. BAM! It hit Goliath right on his forehead.
Goliath crashed to ground.

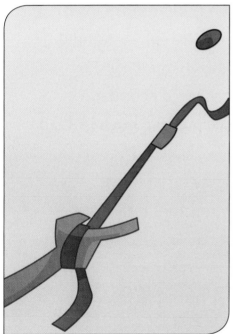

God is bigger than Goliath, right?

Yes, Otto. God is bigger than everyone and everything.

Kings David and Solomon

2 SAMUEL 7:1-17; 1 KINGS 2:10-12; 6

King David lived in a beautiful palace. Outside was the dusty canvas tent where the people had worshipped God for years. Next to David's home, the tent looked old and ragged.

"God, I want to build you a NEW house even GREATER than my own!" King David exclaimed. He rushed to his table to draw a house for God.

"Wait," God said to David. David stopped drawing. "Someday I will have a great house," God said, "but not right now."

"But when?" David asked.

"After you are gone, your son will build my house," God answered. David frowned. How long would THAT be?

"Don't worry," God said. "I promise to ALWAYS stay with you and your people."

David told his son Solomon about God's promise. "One day, YOU will build God's house," David said to Solomon.

After King David died, Solomon became king.

I know how Solomon feels. My parents are always signing me up to do things.

Nothing like building a giant temple for God though, right?

King Solomon remembered God's promise and his father's drawings. It was time to build a house for God!

? ?
What do you like to build?

"Bring me the BEST builders in the land," Solomon directed. "Find the finest STONES and WOOD and GOLD!"

The builders stacked the stones. Walls grew up, up, up! But SHH! Solomon wanted God's house to be a quiet place. No noisy tools allowed!

"This already feels like a holy place," the builders whispered as they worked.

After SEVEN years, the temple in Jerusalem was finished.

Inside the temple, the walls and floor and furniture sparkled with gold. King Solomon smiled. THIS was just like the house his father, David, wanted to build for God. Whenever the people worshipped in this temple, they would remember God's promise to ALWAYS be with them.

Seven years! I could build SO MANY robots in that amount of time.

Yeah, but would all of them work?

Elijah and Elisha

2 KINGS 2:1-15

Elisha knew God would soon take his teacher, Elijah, to heaven. But there was still so much Elisha needed to learn!

Elisha wanted to be a great prophet and leader like his teacher. So he followed Elijah everywhere. He watched Elijah care for God's people. He listened to Elijah share God's messages.

? ?
Who is someone you want to be like when you grow up?

"What can I do for you before I leave to be with God?" Elijah asked Elisha.

Elisha thought and thought. He wanted Elijah to stay much longer. "Please share your spirit with me," Elisha said.

His teacher responded, "You have asked a hard thing. If you watch me as I'm being taken up to heaven, you will receive my spirit."

Ee-lie-JAH and Ee-lie-SHA sound a lot alike.

But only one of them rode in a chariot of fire!

As the two walked and talked, a chariot of fire whooshed down from the sky!

"Father, Father!" Elisha shouted. The chariot and its horses rode between them. The wind was strong. It twisted and blew! The wind ROARED! Elisha covered his ears. The wind stung his eyes. But Elisha didn't stop watching.

The strong wind and the chariot of fire carried Elijah up to heaven!

Elisha's teacher was gone. But the next moment, Elisha felt his teacher's spirit enter HIM.

Elisha felt brave and strong. He stood tall.

That day ELISHA became a leader, too.

Best. Exit. Ever.

Queen Esther

ESTHER 2:5-18; 3:1-6; 8:1-17

"Bow down to ME!" shouted Haman. Haman felt BIG and POWERFUL. King Ahasuerus had put Haman in charge of the WHOLE kingdom.

Knees. Hands. Heads. EVERY servant and advisor bowed down to Haman.

Everyone . . . EXCEPT Mordecai!

Mordecai looked left. He looked right. He was the only person still standing.

"Mordecai," whispered a servant, "bow down!"

Mordecai refused. "I ONLY bow down to GOD."

Haman glared at Mordecai. "Bow down to ME or I will destroy YOU and ALL the other Jewish people!"

Mordecai did NOT bow down. Instead, he RAN to tell his cousin, Queen Esther.

? ?
What can you do when you see a bully?

Why would a king put someone else in charge of everything?

Haman tricked King Ahasuerus (uh-has-you-AIR-us) into signing new laws.

"Queen Esther! Cousin!" Mordecai panted. "Haman plans to destroy ALL the Jewish people! You, me, and every one of our friends and family!"

Esther gasped.

"You MUST tell the king!" Mordecai insisted.

Esther knew her husband, King Ahasuerus, put Haman in charge of laws. She wondered if the king could change Haman's mind.

The queen fell to the ground in front of the king. "Please help," she pleaded. "Haman is going to destroy me, Mordecai, and all our people!"

"Why?" asked the king.

Queen Esther peered up at the king. "We are Jewish. We ONLY bow down to GOD. Haman is angry and wants to hurt us."

The king loved Queen Esther.

"Stand up," he ordered. "I will not allow Haman to destroy your people!"

Queen Esther sighed with relief. Her people were SAFE.

Haman had better watch out! It's dangerous to cross both the king AND the queen!

The Lord Is My Shepherd

PSALM 23

Here is a song about God's peace, written by
King David:

God cares for me like a shepherd cares for sheep,
With food and water and safety.
I love being a sheep in God's flock!
God gives me safe places to rest and grow strong,
Like green fields and calm lakes.

? ?
Where are your safe places?

God is ALWAYS with me.
When I'm in a dark valley and can't see, I'm not afraid!
When I feel lonely, God keeps me company.
When I feel unsure, God reaches out and comforts me.

I will NEVER forget—God's way is the best!

ANOTHER story about a shepherd and sheep?

Lots of people took care of sheep in Bible times. Even King David! He was a shepherd before he was king.

When I'm surrounded by enemies,
God serves up a banquet!
It's a table filled with food for EVERYONE.

Anyone who wants to hurt me will see
God pours out love on me.

God's LOVE always surrounds me.
It's like a cup spilling over because it's so full.

Everywhere I look, I see God's goodness.
Not just today, not just on the good days.
EVERY day!

Wherever I am, God is by my side.

That's a lovely song.

Yeah. But it could use a little more electric guitar.

Isaiah's Message

ISAIAH 2:1-5

The prophet Isaiah spoke God's words. Some messages were comforting. Others challenging. One exciting message was about God's FUTURE. "The Lord is building a BIG house!"

"HOW big?" one woman wondered.

"Bigger than the tallest mountain!" Isaiah exclaimed. "Big enough for EVERYONE! Old people, young people, boys and girls! ALL of them will say, 'Let's GO to the Lord's house! The Lord will teach us how to choose what's right.'"

"Let's go NOW!" one boy called. He raced ahead of Isaiah.

Many people were filled with joy when they heard God's message! They danced and clapped their hands.

? ?
What do you do when you're filled with joy?

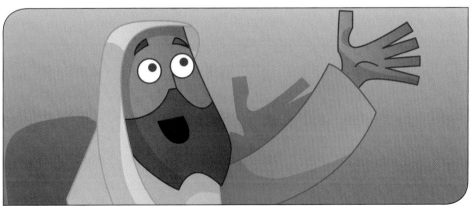

I love a big house! But will it have a pool in the backyard?

I'm sure God's pool would have room for all.

Isaiah hurried along the road to the temple. He shared God's message with ALL the people.

"The Lord will be like a judge—listening to problems and SOLVING them!"

"Can I live in the Lord's house?" a little girl wondered.

"ALL people will be HAPPY! They'll use their swords for garden rakes. Their spears will be weeding tools! NO fighting allowed!"

Children skipped behind Isaiah. They wanted to hear more about a place with NO fighting at all!

Isaiah invited them to follow. "The Lord will teach us how to choose what's right. COME! Let's walk in the light of the Lord!"

It sounds so nice. But they should just buy real rakes. Sword-rakes wouldn't work well at all!

God Calls Jeremiah

JEREMIAH 1:4-10

My name is Jeremiah. I'm one of God's prophets! God gives me messages to share with lots of people.

I didn't choose to be a prophet. God PICKED me.

When I was a boy, I thought I'd be a carpenter. Or a shepherd. I never thought I'd be a prophet! I talked to my family. I talked to my friends. I never imagined God would call me to speak to all God's people!

? ?
What do you want to do someday?

God knew I'd be a prophet—even BEFORE I was born. How does God do that? Even my PARENTS didn't know anything about me before I was born!

Wow! One of God's prophets was a kid, just like us!

God knew that Jeremiah could do it.

When God told me I was going to be a prophet, I was afraid. I didn't know how to speak. Who would listen to me? I was just a KID!

God told me not to be afraid. So I tried to be brave! God promised to give me the words to say. And God did! God told me the people would listen. And they did!

I've brought God's word to grown-ups and kings as well as kids and common people. I've delivered God's messages—happy and sad, long and short!

I know that EVERY time I speak to God's people, God is with me.

When God calls kids to do something, kids can do it!

Daniel and the Lions

DANIEL 6

Daniel tumbled into the pit. Hungry lions paced around him. Daniel couldn't escape. King Darius couldn't save him. Only GOD could keep the lions away.

King Darius's advisors didn't like Daniel. They made a law they knew Daniel would break.

"Everyone must pray only to King Darius," the law stated. "If you don't, you'll be thrown to the lions!"

Daniel respected King Darius. But Daniel prayed ONLY to God.

The king's advisors caught Daniel praying to God. "To the LIONS!" they shouted.

King Darius liked Daniel. "How can I save him?" the king wondered.

But even the king could not change the law.

I thought being a king would be fun. But if lions can still eat your friends, it doesn't sound so good.

The lions in the pit watched Daniel. They growled and licked their lips. Daniel closed his eyes. He tried not to think of the lions' sharp teeth.

"God," Daniel prayed, "you are faithful. Keep me safe."

? ?
When do you pray?

Daniel's eyes opened. An angel appeared in the pit. The angel SNAPPED the lions' mouths SHUT.

The lions were confused. They whimpered through closed lips. They pawed at their stuck mouths.

Daniel turned his eyes to God. "Thank you, LORD!" he cried out.

Early in the morning, King Darius shouted into the pit, "Daniel?"

"I'm here!" Daniel shouted back.

"Your God protects you!" King Darius exclaimed. "I'll make a new law. Everyone must honor the faithfulness of Daniel's God!"

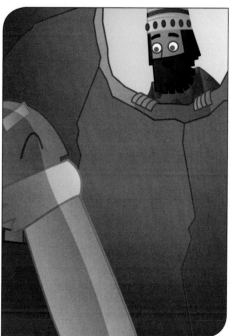

That was a close one! And God was faithful to Daniel by protecting him even in the lions' den.

Being faithful means being loyal. Daniel prayed faithfully, even when it was dangerous.

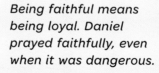

Jonah and the Big Fish

JONAH 1; 2:1-2, 10; 3:1-5, 10

Jonah was a prophet, but he didn't feel like God's messenger. As he crawled up the beach, he felt slimy and smelled like fish.

"JONAH!" God's voice boomed. "Go tell the people in Nineveh I'm angry at the way they are living."

Jonah groaned. God had asked him to do this before, but Jonah was sure the people would not listen. He tried to run away, but God had him swallowed by a giant fish. It was dark and lonely in the belly of the fish. It was very stinky and very wet. After three days and three nights Jonah decided to pray to God.

The fish spit him out here on the sandy beach, where God spoke to him again. Jonah covered his ears, but he could still hear God. "Jonah! GO TO NINEVEH!"

A fish that big MUST have been stinky!

Jonah brushed off the sticky sand. Running away again wouldn't work. He didn't want to go, but he needed to do what God asked. He dragged himself to Nineveh.

? ?
What is something you don't like to do?

Jonah stomped into the city shouting, "In forty days God will destroy you!" There. He did it. Now God would leave him alone.

But the people in Nineveh surprised Jonah. They listened to God's message!

"We are sorry," they prayed to God. "Give us another chance! We will change the way we're living."

God saw what they did.

God did not destroy Nineveh.

Jonah got a second chance to listen to God, and so did the people of Nineveh.

Sounds like a do-over. I love it when I get a do-over!

Malachi's Message

MALACHI 3:1-4

The people in Jerusalem call me *my messenger*.

? ?
What names are you called?

Whose messenger am I? GOD'S messenger!

When I open MY mouth, GOD speaks.
MY words are GOD'S words.

God called many messengers before me:
Isaiah, Jeremiah, Daniel, and Jonah, to name a few.

We are all called *prophets*.
I am also called *my messenger*.

I delivered MANY messages
to God's people, the Israelites.
Sometimes the Israelites forgot
to follow God's commandments.
Sometimes they forgot how to worship God.

So God asked ME to be a messenger to remind them.

How could the Israelites forget God's Commandments? There are only ten!

People aren't perfect. I'll bet you have broken a commandment.

Maybe . . .

This is what I told them.

Listen up! God has a message for YOU.
It's time to get ready!
God promised you a Messiah.
And the Messiah will come!

But you aren't ready!
You break God's commandments.
You work on the Sabbath.
You steal and lie.
STOP what you're doing and CHANGE!

Like SOAP makes cloth clean,
God will make YOU clean.
Like FIRE purifies silver, God will purify YOU.
All your mistakes will be washed away!
God will forgive ALL your sins!
God will forgive EVERYONE!

Prepare the way!
Follow God's commandments.
Be kind to each other.
Share your things and love your neighbors.
Then you'll be READY for God's Messiah!

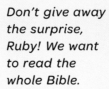

Oh, he's talking about the Messiah coming! I know who that is!

Don't give away the surprise, Ruby! We want to read the whole Bible.

The Annunciation

MATTHEW 1:18-25   **LUKE 1:26-38**

WHOOSH! Who was THAT? Mary jumped in surprise and tried to hide. She was expecting Joseph to visit her to talk about their wedding. But it wasn't Joseph. It was an angel named Gabriel with a message from God!

"Don't be afraid!" Gabriel announced. "I have good news for you. You will have a baby! His name will be Jesus. He will be YOUR son, but he will also be GOD'S Son."

"How is this possible?" Mary asked.

Gabriel answered her, "The Holy Spirit makes all things possible. Your child will be holy, the Messiah, the savior for God's people."

Mary was scared, but excited, too. She took a deep breath and stood up tall. "Here I am," she said. "I will love and care for God's Son."

Mary rushed to tell Joseph the news.

I wonder why angels almost always start out by saying, "Don't be afraid."

I wonder why Mary tried to hide at first. I would LOVE to see an angel!

Joseph tossed and turned in his sleep. He was worried about Mary's news. Mary was going to have a baby? God's Son? While Joseph slept, God sent Gabriel to bring him a message, too.

"Don't be afraid!" Gabriel said. "God wants you to care for this baby. You will name him Jesus. He will be a descendant of King David. But he will also be a king for God's people."

Joseph woke up, amazed by his dream. Gabriel was gone, but he remembered the good news. Soon he and Mary would be married. Together they would love and care for God's own Son!

? ?
Who loves and cares for you?

It's sort of like God asked Joseph to be the stepdad to Jesus.

Good thing Joseph stepped up to the job.

Mary's Song

LUKE 1:39-55

Mary hummed as she walked to her cousin Elizabeth's house. She was excited to share the good news with Elizabeth. Mary was going to have a baby. Not just any baby. God's Son, Jesus!

Mary stood outside Elizabeth's home. Knock, knock, knock! Elizabeth opened the door. Elizabeth's belly was big and round. Even though Elizabeth was much older than Mary, God had blessed her with a child too.

"Surprise!" Mary sang.

Elizabeth wrapped her arms around Mary. "You are blessed!" Elizabeth exclaimed. "You will be the mother of God's Son! When I heard your voice, my baby jumped for joy inside of me! You are blessed because you heard God's words and believed."

Elizabeth's baby was John the Baptist. Since Mary and Elizabeth were cousins, John the Baptist and Jesus were cousins too!

Sometimes I think having a cousin is better than having a sister.

138

Mary was filled with joy. She took a deep breath and sang a beautiful song of praise to God.

Day after day, year after year,
God is good! Oh so good!
God is always good!
God is doing amazing things,
And I am blessed indeed!

Day after day, year after year,
God fills us with good things.
God's love is wild and fierce.
God is turning the world upside down,
And so I dance and sing!

? ?
When do you like to dance and sing?

God does amazing things!

Jesus Is Born

LUKE 2:1-20

Mary and Joseph packed quickly. They needed to go to Bethlehem to be counted by the emperor.

Mary was worried. Where would they stay? Joseph was concerned. Would they be gone a long time? Mary and Joseph were BOTH excited. Soon their son Jesus would be born!

Bethlehem was crowded with people. Knock, knock! Mary and Joseph knocked on door after door. There was nowhere for them to stay! Squeeze! Mary grabbed Joseph's hand tight. The baby was coming!

That night, Mary gave birth to a tiny baby. It was Jesus! Joseph found a simple wooden manger for Jesus' bed. Mary wrapped her newborn son tightly in cloth and laid him on the golden hay.

The baby Jesus yawned with his tiny mouth. Joseph touched his tiny fingers. Mary looked at his tiny, wrinkled face and smiled.

I love babies! I don't like stinky diapers or crying in the middle of the night, but I love babies!

I would wrap Jesus in a soft yellow blanket like Mom said she did for me.

In a nearby field, shepherds watched the starry sky in the quiet night. A bright light FLASHED! The shepherds JUMPED! An angel appeared. The shepherds tried to hide.

"Don't be afraid!" the angel said. "I have GOOD news! Tonight the Messiah was born. God's Son has come to be with you. His name is Jesus."

A choir of angels filled the sky. The shepherds were AMAZED! The angels' song echoed across the hills. "Glory to God! Peace on earth!"

? ?

What Christmas songs do you know?

The shepherds hurried to see Jesus. Then they raced across the hills shouting the good news.

"Jesus is BORN!"

I wonder if the light in the sky looked like fireworks, lightning, or a giant spotlight.

Simeon and Anna

LUKE 2:22-40

Simeon and Anna were prophets. God spoke to them in dreams and visions so they could share God's messages with people.

But sometimes they had to wait a long time for God's promises to happen.

God told Simeon he would meet the Messiah. THAT was something worth waiting for! So Simeon waited. He grew older. And he waited. His hair turned gray, and he began walking more slowly.

And STILL Simeon waited.

? ?
What have you waited for?

Anna prayed in the temple. Hearing God was something worth waiting for. So Anna prayed. She got older. And she prayed. Her face got wrinkles, and her eyesight got worse.

And STILL Anna prayed.

I bet I could wait as long as they did!

Otto, you can hardly wait for your dessert after dinner.

While Simeon was waiting for the Messiah, he saw a mother and father with their baby coming to the temple.

It was the Messiah! It was Jesus! Simeon's waiting was over. He hurried to meet Jesus and his parents, Mary and Joseph.

Simeon took Jesus in his arms and blessed him. Mary and Joseph were amazed. "Thank you, God!" Simeon shouted. Anna heard Simeon's shout and came to see why he was so excited.

"God, you told me I would meet the Messiah!" Simeon said. "This boy will bring light to everyone, everywhere!"

Anna praised God and started telling people about Jesus, God's Son.

Baby Jesus and his parents returned to their town where he grew and learned and became strong.

The people of Israel believed God lived in the temple.

Does that mean Jesus had two homes growing up?

The Wise Men

MATTHEW 2:1-12

Far away from Bethlehem, wise men studied the night sky. In the distance, they spotted a new star—bigger and brighter than all the rest!

"That bigger, brighter star means a NEW king is BORN!" said one of the wise men. "Let's go find and welcome him!"

The wise men left on a LONG journey, following the star.

In Jerusalem, they met King Herod.

"We're looking for the NEW king," the wise men told King Herod.

"I don't know ANYTHING about a NEW king," Herod said nervously. "What do YOU know?"

"Only that there's a new star in the sky that's bigger and brighter than all the rest," they replied.

"When you find this NEW king," said Herod, "come tell me where he is. I would like to honor him.

I don't trust this King Herod. He seems like he's up to something . . .

You're an excellent judge of character!

The bigger and brighter star led the wise men to a little home in Bethlehem.

Knock, knock! A father opened the door.

"May we see the NEW king?" they asked. "We want to WELCOME him!"

A child peeked out from behind his father, Joseph.

"He's WONDERFUL!" said one of the wise men.

"What's his name?" whispered another.

"Jesus," said the boy's mother, Mary.

"A gift for the world!" announced the third wise man.

At the end of their visit, the wise men left three gifts to honor Jesus—gold, frankincense, and myrrh.

? ?

What gift would you bring to Jesus?

That night in a dream, the wise men were warned that King Herod wanted to be the ONLY king. They decided NOT to tell Herod where the NEW king was. Instead they returned home by another route so King Herod couldn't find Jesus.

What's a baby going to do with presents like THAT?

If he didn't want them, I'd be happy to take them.

Escape to Egypt

MATTHEW 2:13-23

Joseph tossed and turned in his sleep. An angel of the Lord appeared in his dream with an important message about his family.

"GET UP!" the angel urged. "King Herod wants to hurt Jesus. Wake your family. Escape to Egypt! Stay there until I tell you it's safe to come back."

Joseph's heart pounded. He jumped up and tried to rub the sleep from his eyes. Frantically, he shook Mary's shoulder. "Wake up! We have to leave. Our baby, Jesus, is in danger."

Joseph packed his heavy carpenter's tools. Mary carried little Jesus. The family escaped into the dark night.

Isn't Egypt where the other Joseph with the coat and the brothers stayed for a while?

Yes, Egypt was the place to go when things were tough in Israel.

In Egypt, Mary, Joseph, and Jesus were safe. Joseph worked as a carpenter. Jesus learned to walk and talk and play. Mary worried about their family and friends in Israel.

? ?
How many times has your family moved?

One night, the angel of the Lord reappeared in Joseph's dream. "King Herod is dead. It's safe to go back home."

Joseph woke Mary and Jesus.

"Hallelujah!" Joseph praised God. "We're going home to Israel." Jesus clapped and Mary danced.

In the bright light of day, the family returned home. Joseph packed his tools. Mary carried their food. Jesus was moving to a new home.

They returned to the little town called Nazareth where Joseph had grown up.

Hey, I've heard of that town before! Sometimes Jesus is called Jesus of Nazareth.

That's because Jesus grew up there too!

Young Jesus in the Temple

LUKE 2:41-52

Whew! Mary and Joseph were exhausted. Their family had spent a WHOLE week in Jerusalem celebrating Passover.

The Passover festival was exciting and busy. The smell of food was everywhere. The air was full of singing. The temple was PACKED with people!

Mary yawned. Finally, they were traveling home.

"Joseph," Mary said, looking around. "Where's Jesus?" He was missing!

"Have you seen Jesus?" they asked aunts and uncles and cousins. "We can't find him!" Nobody knew where Jesus was.

Mary grabbed Joseph's arm. "We have to go back to Jerusalem! We have to find JESUS!"

My mom couldn't find me once when we were at the public library. I wasn't done learning yet.

Mary and Joseph looked near the city gate. No Jesus!

Maybe he was hungry. They ran to the food tents. NO Jesus!

Jesus loved singing! They searched the choirs outside the temple. NO JESUS!

For THREE days, they searched EVERYWHERE. NO JESUS!

Finally, they entered the temple. Mary gasped when she saw him. "There's JESUS!"

Jesus was telling grown-up teachers about God! Mary's and Joseph's eyes grew wide in surprise. The teachers were AMAZED. Jesus was only 12 years old!

"We were so worried!" Mary scolded Jesus. "We searched for you everywhere!"

? ?
When have your parents worried about you?

"Why were you searching for me?" Jesus asked. "Didn't you KNOW I would be in my FATHER'S house?"

Mary and Joseph didn't understand.

Jesus continued to grow and learn.

I'm always trying to teach my teachers important stuff!

I guess you're not as good a teacher as Jesus, Otto.

John the Baptist

MARK 1:1-8

John the Baptist stood tall by the Jordan River. He waved his arms so people could see him. He told the people an important message from God.

"Listen, everybody!" he shouted. "It's time to get ready!"

"Get ready for what?" the people asked. They were confused.

"Get ready for the Messiah!" exclaimed John. "Our king and savior is coming!"

"The Messiah?" asked the people. They were STILL confused. They had so many questions.

For many years, religious leaders and prophets said such a hero would come. Was the Messiah REALLY coming NOW? How did John the Baptist know?

Muss-SIGH-uh? What's that, exactly?

The Jewish people believed God would send the Messiah to save them from their trouble.

162

"Change your life!" said John. "Follow God's rules. Share your things. Love each other. When you make a mistake, ask for forgiveness. Wash away your sins. THAT'S how you get ready!"

God's people were excited. They tried to get ready. They tried to follow God's rules. They shared more and loved more. They asked for forgiveness and forgave others.

People of all ages came to John to be baptized.

John was quite a sight! His camel hair coat was itchy and scratchy. Kids saw him eat BUGS! He dipped them in honey and crunched them up with his teeth. Most important, John baptized everyone by dunking them in the Jordan River.

? ?

How have you seen people be baptized?

"The Messiah is coming!" John said over and over. "Get ready!"

John the Baptist and I have a lot in common. I ate a bug once when I was riding my bike.

Jesus Is Baptized

LUKE 3:15-17, 21-22

"Get ready!" John the Baptist called out. "The Messiah is coming!"

An old man sat on the bank of the Jordan River. "We've been waiting a long time for the Messiah," he grumbled.

A little girl ran up to John. "Maybe YOU are the Messiah!"

"Not me!" said John. "LOOK!" He pointed to a man walking toward them. "I baptize you with water. But HE will baptize you with God's Spirit."

The crowd wondered, "Could THIS be the Messiah?"

The man approached the crowd. It was JESUS!

According to my calculations, people had been waiting generations for the Messiah to arrive.

That's like your great-grandparents waiting for something to happen, and then it finally happens to you!

Jesus waded into the water. John baptized Jesus by dunking him in the river.

When Jesus came out of the water, heaven opened and the crowd heard a voice. They looked around. Where did it come from?

The voice came from nowhere and everywhere all at once. It sounded different to each person.

"God's voice," the little girl whispered.

? ?
What do you think God's voice sounds like?

"YOU are my Son," said the voice. "YOU are the Beloved. With YOU I am well pleased."

The old man pointed. Something flew down from the sky. It looked like a dove. It was God's own Spirit!

The crowd gasped.

THIS was the one they had been waiting for! Jesus was the Messiah. God's own voice said so. God's Spirit was upon him.

Wait, God's Spirit is a bird?

God's Spirit only looked like a bird in this story. The Spirit can look like anything!

Jesus Calls the Disciples

LUKE 5:1-11

"Last time!" Peter shouted. "PULL!" Andrew, James, and John pulled in their fishing nets. Empty AGAIN!

The men slumped in the boat. They fished ALL night but caught NO fish.

? ?
What would you use to try to catch fish?

Slowly, they rowed back to shore. They felt disappointed, tired, and hungry.

Jesus walked up to them and got into the boat. People had gathered on the beach to hear Jesus teach.

As they floated out into the water, Jesus said, "Peter, try your nets ONE more time."

"Teacher," Peter groaned as he lowered the nets, "there are NO fish here."

But Peter felt a tug. And another! The fishermen struggled to pull in the nets. Flopping fish FILLED the boat!

Peter and the others have a lot to learn from Jesus. He's even great at fishing!

"Impossible!" yelled James.

"A miracle!" yelled Andrew.

"Jesus filled our nets with fish!" yelled John.

Peter fell to his knees and whispered, "Leave me alone, Jesus. I don't deserve this miracle from God."

"Don't be afraid," Jesus comforted. "God's miracles are for EVERYONE! Follow me. We won't catch any more fish. We'll catch PEOPLE."

Peter dropped the nets, still wiggling with fish. The fishermen left their boats and followed Jesus.

Jesus caught others along the way. "Matthew! Philip! Bartholomew! Thomas! James! Thaddaeus! Simon! Judas!" Twelve men heard Jesus and followed him as disciples.

Did the men just leave those fish on the beach? Jesus must have known they'd be better disciples than fishermen.

The Beatitudes

MATTHEW 5:1-12

Jesus perched on a rock on the side of a mountain. He peered out over the large crowd below. Raising his arms, Jesus hushed the crowd. All eyes turned to look. All ears were ready to listen.

"If you're sad and lonely, you are BLESSED! God will comfort you," Jesus taught.

The crowd whispered, "We thought happy people were BLESSED."

"If you have little or no money, you are BLESSED. God will give you what you need!"

? ?
How does God give you the things you need?

A poor man looked at his tattered sandals. "I'm BLESSED?" he wondered.

Why is Jesus up on the side of a mountain?

So many people came to see him, he had to climb up high to speak to them all.

"If you want life to be fair for everyone, you are BLESSED! You will see the wonderful way God works," Jesus continued.

A little girl tugged on her mother's sleeve. "God can make life fair?" she asked.

"If you forgive others, you are BLESSED. God will forgive you."

The crowd murmured. "Forgive others? Even people who are unkind?"

"If you get along with others, you are BLESSED! Everyone will know you are a child of God!"

Two women hugged. "We're both children of God!" they exclaimed.

"When people tease you or tell lies about you because you follow me, you are BLESSED! You will live in heaven!"

"HURRAY!" shouted the people. Sad, lonely, poor, kind—Jesus BLESSED them ALL!

So Jesus blessed everybody. Hurray! That means me too!

Love Your Enemies

MATTHEW 5:38-48

The disciples' eyes were wide open. Jesus was teaching SURPRISING things!

"If someone hits your cheek, what should you do?" Jesus asked.

Peter was quick to answer. "Hit them back!"

"NO!" replied Jesus. "If someone hurts you, do not hurt back."

Then Jesus asked, "What if someone tries to take your coat?"

The disciples scratched their heads. "Take THEIR coat?" asked Thomas.

Jesus shook his head. "Let them have your coat. And your cloak and sandals too. Give everything you have."

"What?" wondered Andrew. "That's not FAIR!"

But Jesus wasn't teaching about FAIRNESS. Jesus was teaching about LOVE.

If someone takes your coat, don't take their coat. That's just trading coats!

"Did Moses tell you to love your neighbor?"
Jesus asked.

? ?
Who are your neighbors?

The disciples were quiet. Peter looked at Andrew. Andrew looked at James. James shrugged. "Yes?" he guessed.

"Yes!" Jesus answered. James smiled a big smile.

"But you have to love your enemies too!" Jesus said. "Pray for them. Love them like God loves them."

The disciples frowned. "Love our enemies?" Philip asked. "Our enemies are unkind to us! How can we love them?"

"It's easy to love the people who love you," Jesus said. "It's not easy to love the people who don't love you. God loves EVERYONE. Practice loving like God does."

Jesus knew about having enemies. Lots of people didn't like what he was saying.

The Lord's Prayer

MATTHEW 6:5-15

Jesus looked down, down, down the mountainside. A huge crowd looked up, up, up at him. The people were waiting to hear Jesus teach about prayer.

"Talk with God!" said Jesus. "That's what PRAYER is. TALKING with God. And LISTENING for God."

"Dear God, I'm hungry!" a little boy squeaked. His mother frowned and shushed him.

"It's OKAY to tell God you're hungry!" Jesus said. "God wants to hear from you!

? ?
What do you talk about with God?

"Talk with God when you're alone or in a group. Talk out loud, in a whisper, or in your head. Fold your hands and close your eyes, or take a walk and listen for God.

"The IMPORTANT thing is to PRAY.

"When you're angry or sad, when you're happy or excited, when you're worried or afraid, PRAY!"

So talking to God a lot is good, but talking on my cell phone all the time is bad?

I know it's a lot to keep track of, Ruby.

Some people in the crowd closed their eyes. Some looked up to the sky. Some folded their hands. But nobody started praying.

"What should we say first?" a young woman asked.

"Begin like this: Our Father in heaven," said Jesus. "Then thank God for the good things in your life. ALL good things come from God."

"Thanks for family!" a father said.

"Thanks for our teacher!" a disciple called out.

"Can you thank God for God?" a child asked.

"YES! That's called PRAISING God," said Jesus.

"Ask for what you need each day," Jesus continued. "Ask God to forgive you for the things you've done wrong. Ask for help forgiving people who have done wrong things to you.

"Remember," Jesus said, "you can talk with God about ANYTHING."

"ANYTHING?" the people asked.

Jesus smiled. "ANYTHING! And EVERYTHING!"

But what if I pray for something and don't get it? Did God miss the message?

No, God's always listening, even if we don't get everything we want.

Don't Worry about Tomorrow

MATTHEW 6:24-34

Jesus' followers looked worried. "What's wrong?" Jesus asked them.

"I'm worried about my family having enough food," a man answered. "If we run out, what will we eat?"

"I'm worried about this hole in my scarf," added a woman. "If it falls apart, what will I wear?"

? ?
Who do you tell when you are worried?

"Listen," Jesus said to his followers. "What do you hear?"

Everyone closed their eyes and listened. "Birds chirping and whistling!" a little boy said.

Worrying gives me a bad feeling in my stomach and makes my neck all tight.

"Birds eat seeds and nuts and worms. Do birds save their food in a barn to eat later?" Jesus asked.

"Of course not." Jesus' followers grinned.

"God provides food for those little birds. Won't God provide food for you?"

Jesus pointed to a field of flowers. "Look at the lilies. What colors do you see?"

"Orange! Pink! Yellow! Blue!" the crowd called out.

"Even rich kings don't wear so many beautiful colors!" Jesus exclaimed. "Do you think these flowers worry about what colors they'll wear?"

"No!" laughed the followers.

"God clothes these flowers in beautiful colors. Won't God give you clothes to wear?"

Jesus continued, "God loves you more than birds or flowers. God knows you need food and clothing. Don't worry TODAY about what might happen TOMORROW. Seek God's WILL. Trust God's LOVE."

God isn't going to try to feed me worms and make me wear flowers, right?

No, I think God knows you a little better than that.

The Parable of the Sower

MATTHEW 13:1-9, 18-23

Jesus loved to teach people. Sometimes Jesus taught in a house. Sometimes he taught in a temple. But TODAY Jesus was teaching next to a sea.

"I have a story for you!" Jesus said.

"A sower went out to sow some seeds.

"Did he plant the seeds in a pretty pot? NO!

"Did he plant the seeds in a long, straight row? He did NOT!

"He flung the seeds EVERYWHERE!

"Some seeds landed on a smooth path, but birds flew down and gobbled them up.

"Other seeds fell on rocky ground, but the hot sun burned the tiny green sprouts.

"Other seeds nested in thick, thorny bushes, but they choked the little seeds.

"But SOME seeds nestled in GOOD soil and grew into BIG, STRONG plants. The healthy plants grew MORE seeds. There were seeds EVERYWHERE!"

? ?
Have you ever planted seeds? What grew?

Wait, I thought a sower made clothes!

No, sowing is when you plant seeds. Sewing is making clothes.

Jesus looked at the crowd. Some heads nodded up and down. Others shook side to side. Some people smiled. Others frowned. Jesus realized they didn't understand yet.

"The sower is like God," Jesus said.

"But the sower is so messy!" a little boy shouted. "He flung his seeds EVERYWHERE!"

Jesus laughed. "God doesn't mind being messy."

"Does God care where we plant our seeds?" a mother asked.

Jesus shook his head. "God trusts farmers to plant seeds," he replied. "I'm talking about how God gives LOVE to you."

"The sower has a LOT of seed," said a grandfather. "He shares it far and wide. Is God like that?"

Jesus smiled. "God shows abundant love to the WHOLE world," he said. "Hear this good news and let it grow in your ears and your hearts: God's love is EVERYWHERE!"

I'm glad to know God's okay with my messy room.

I don't think that's what Jesus meant, Otto.

Jesus Walks on Water

MATTHEW 14:22-33

Twelve disciples floated in a boat on the lake. Jesus was not with them.

As the sun set, the wind began to blow. WHOOSH! The wind blew harder. SPLASH! Big waves pushed the little boat back and forth, up and down. The frightened disciples grabbed onto the boat and tried not to fall overboard.

? ?
What is it like to be in a boat?

All through the night, the little boat was rocked and knocked and pushed by the wind. The disciples floated far, far away from the shore.

Early in the morning, the disciples spotted someone walking near the boat, ON TOP of the water!

"It's a GHOST!" John screamed.

Everyone ducked into the bottom of the boat to hide.

I've SKIED on water, but never walked.

"Don't be afraid," the disciples heard a calm voice say. "It's me."

One by one, twelve pairs of eyes peeked over the side of the boat. It was JESUS! Walking ON the WATER!

"Jesus, if it's really you," Peter called, "tell me to walk ON the WATER to you."

"Come to me, Peter," said Jesus.

Carefully, Peter stuck one foot out. It didn't sink! He stuck the other foot out. It didn't sink either! He stood up. He did it! Peter was walking ON the WATER!

WHOOSH! The wind blew. SPLASH! A wave crashed. Peter was afraid! He began to sink. First his feet were covered in water, then his legs, then his belly button! Peter couldn't swim.

"Jesus, help me!" Peter shouted.

Jesus grabbed Peter's hand. "Why did you doubt?" he asked Peter.

When they climbed back into the boat, the wind stopped blowing. Amazed, the disciples dropped to their knees and worshipped Jesus, saying, "YOU are God's SON."

Peter couldn't swim? But he was a fisherman!

Fishermen are supposed to stay in the boat.

Jesus Teaches about Forgiveness

MATTHEW 18:21-35

"Jesus," Peter asked, "if someone is unkind to me, how many times should I forgive? One time? Two times? Seven times?"

"Not one, two, or seven times, but 70 TIMES seven," Jesus replied.

Peter started to count to 490. That was a LOT of times! "But why, Jesus?" he asked.

Jesus looked with kind eyes at his friend. "We forgive each other because we love each other."

? ?

What happens after you say, "I'm sorry," to someone?

Then Jesus told Peter a story about forgiveness.

70 X 7 used to be as far as numbers went. After that they just said, "A whole bunch."

I don't think that's right . . .

A man owed his king a lot of money. The man worked hard to pay his debt, but it wasn't enough. He worked even harder, but it STILL wasn't enough. "Please give me more time," he begged.

The king showed love to the man. He told him, "You don't have to pay me. I forgive your debt."

The man raced home to share his good news!

On the way home, the man met one of his friends. "YOU owe ME money!" he shouted. His friend couldn't pay the debt. The man became angry and threw his friend in prison.

When the king heard this, he felt frustrated. He told the man, "I forgave YOU because you asked me and I showed mercy. Choose to forgive and love others like I did for you."

The man doesn't sound like a real friend. I think I'll tell Otto he doesn't owe me two dollars anymore.

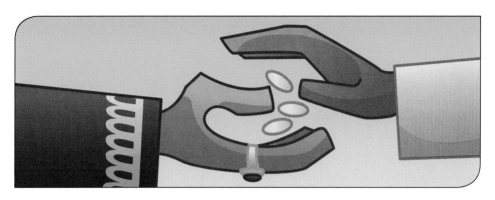

The Parable of the Vineyard

MATTHEW 20:1-16

The early morning sun was shining on a vineyard full of plump, juicy grapes. The vineyard owner saw that the grapes were ripe and ready to be picked. At 9 o'clock he hired hardworking men to pick the grapes. The workers picked and picked, but STILL there were more grapes!

? ?
What color grapes do you like?

At 12 o'clock, the vineyard owner hired more workers. They picked and picked, but STILL there were more grapes!

At 3 o'clock AND 5 o'clock, the vineyard owner hired even MORE workers. They picked and picked and PICKED.

Finally, there were no more grapes.

I wonder why it's called a vineyard instead of a grape patch.

The sun set. Time to pay all the workers!

The vineyard owner paid the workers who started at 5 o'clock FIRST. He paid the workers who started at 9 o'clock LAST. Every worker got the SAME amount!

The early morning workers grumbled. "WHAT? We worked all day! We picked the most grapes! No fair! Why are the afternoon workers paid the same?"

The vineyard owner replied, "I paid you what I promised you. Can't I give away what is mine any way I want?"

Jesus wanted to teach people about God's kingdom. "Like the vineyard owner who surprised EVERYONE by giving the LAST the same as the FIRST," Jesus said, "God is more generous than ANYONE can imagine!"

The last workers hired were paid first? I'd want to start working at 5 o'clock!

That's not surprising, Otto. Jesus told LOTS of stories about God's kingdom having unexpected surprises.

Jesus and the Pharisees

MATTHEW 22:15-22

The Pharisees loved the religious rules. They studied Jewish law and wanted to be important leaders. They were always looking for people who broke the rules. But the crowd wasn't paying attention to them!

"Everyone is listening to Jesus instead of US!" they grumbled. "How can we show the crowd they shouldn't listen to Jesus?"

They decided to create a trap. Asking Jesus a tricky riddle would get him in trouble!

"Say, Jesus," the Pharisees started. "The emperor says we should give our money to HIM. Other people say that's NOT what God wants. Who is right? The emperor? Or God?"

I have a whole book of riddles! I guarantee Jesus could answer all of them without even looking in the back.

If Jesus said the emperor, then people would think he wasn't following God. If Jesus said God, he would go to jail for disobeying the emperor.

Jesus picked up a shiny coin. "Look!" he said. "This has a picture on it. Who is that?"

He held up the coin.

? ?

Whose picture do you see on coins?

"The emperor," the Pharisees answered. That was an easy question!

"Then the emperor can have this coin," Jesus replied.

Trapped! Jesus loved the emperor more than God!

"But wait!" Jesus added. "This is more important: Whose image is on YOU?"

The Pharisees were stumped. If people are made in God's image, then EVERYONE belongs to God.

Jesus answered a question with a question!

I enjoy the fact that Jesus is good at playing with words.

The Greatest Commandment

MATTHEW 22:34-40

The Pharisees spent a lot of time learning about God's law. They were ALWAYS testing Jesus with hard questions. But WHY?

Maybe the Pharisees wanted to prove they knew the most about God. Maybe some wanted to get Jesus in trouble for saying the wrong thing. Maybe some wanted to follow Jesus, but only if he agreed with them about God's law.

Jesus was teaching a crowd of Pharisees and scribes in the temple. A Pharisee who was a lawyer stood bravely in front of Jesus. The lawyer wanted to ask him an important question about God's law.

"Jesus," the lawyer asked, "which of God's commandments is NUMBER ONE?"

What's the Pharisees' problem?

Some people have a harder time believing. But everyone can eventually.

"I'll give you TWO answers," said Jesus. "FIRST, love God with THREE parts of yourself: your heart, your soul, and your mind."

"NEXT," Jesus added, "love your neighbor— EVERY neighbor—the way you love yourself."

? ?

How do you show love to your neighbors?

One of the scribes jumped up from the crowd. He rushed to stand in front of Jesus. "Loving God and each other is number one! Love is the most important of ALL God's commandments!"

Jesus smiled because the scribe understood.

After that, no one asked Jesus any more tricky questions.

Hey! The Pharisees asked for one rule, but Jesus gave two!

But he did answer their questions.

Serving People, Serving Jesus

MATTHEW 25:31-46

"Jesus, how do you know who serves you and who doesn't?" the disciples wondered.

"I know who serves me like a shepherd knows his sheep," Jesus explained. "A shepherd knows how to tell a sheep from a goat. People who serve me are like my sheep. People who don't are like goats."

"We want to be like the sheep!" the disciples said eagerly. "HOW can we serve you?"

"When you serve OTHER people, you serve ME." Jesus smiled. "When you feed someone who is hungry, you serve me. When you share your blanket with someone who is cold, you serve me. When you care for someone who is sick, you serve me."

The disciples looked pleased with themselves. Of COURSE they knew how to serve Jesus.

I wonder why it was so important to tell the difference between sheep and goats.

Well, they did call Jesus the Good Shepherd, not the Good Goatherd.

"But," Jesus warned, "when people do NOT serve others, they do NOT serve me. Every time you ignore someone who needs your help, it is like ignoring me, too."

Uh-oh. The disciples looked at each other. They felt nervous as they started thinking about if they had ignored someone who needed help.

"How can we be sure to ALWAYS serve you, Jesus?" they asked.

"Help others! Share! Love each other!" Jesus replied. "God's kingdom is for those who show their love by serving others in need."

? ?
What's your favorite way to serve others?

But can I ignore someone if I can't think of how to serve them?

That's NOT what Jesus means, Otto.

216

Healing at Simon's House

MARK 1:29-39

Jesus, James, and John went to visit their friend Simon. KNOCK, KNOCK, KNOCK. Simon answered the door. He looked worried. "What's wrong, Simon?" asked James.

Simon answered, "My wife's mother is very sick. She's in bed with a fever."

? ?
Who helps when you're sick?

Simon knew Jesus healed people. "Jesus, will you help her?" he asked.

Jesus nodded. He walked over to Simon's mother-in-law, held her hand, and lifted her up.

Suddenly, her fever was gone! She jumped out of bed to serve her guests.

Later that night, the whole town gathered outside Simon's house. Jesus stayed up late to heal many who were sick, hurt, or filled with unclean spirits.

Our dad has a mother-in-law. She's our mom's mom. We call her Grandma.

It must be cool to have a double name like Simon Peter. He could be called Simon, or Peter, or Simon Peter!

Before the sun came up in the morning, Jesus went out and found a place to be alone and pray.

When Jesus' friends woke up, they couldn't find Jesus anywhere. Everyone looked for Jesus. Simon looked for Jesus. James and John looked for Jesus. Simon's mother-in-law looked for Jesus. The whole town looked for Jesus.

Finally, Simon found him! "Jesus," said Simon, "everyone's been looking for you!"

Jesus told Simon, "It's time to go teach and heal MORE people in other towns."

If Jesus played hide-and-seek, I bet he'd win!

A Man through a Roof

MARK 2:1-12

"One, two, three, LIFT!" shouted four friends together. They each grabbed a corner of the mat and lifted up their friend who was paralyzed. One step at a time, they began their journey to find Jesus. The four friends were filled with hope. Maybe Jesus could heal their friend's legs so he could walk again.

After many miles, the friends spotted a BIG crowd surrounding a LITTLE house in the distance. "That must be where Jesus is!" they exclaimed.

? ?

What is the biggest crowd you have ever seen?

At the edge of the crowd, the four friends began to worry.

"This crowd is too big!" one said. "We can't get THROUGH it!"

"There are too many people!" another added. "We can't go AROUND them!"

"I have an idea!" a third yelled. "Let's go OVER them! To the roof!"

It took four people to carry this guy? Was he a football player?

No, but they had to carry him a long way.

Inside the house, Jesus was teaching about God.

THUMP! Jesus stopped teaching. BOOM! A crack appeared in the ceiling. CRASH! Chunks of mud dropped to the ground as the roof CAVED IN. Four faces peeked inside through a BIG hole. "It's Jesus!" they exclaimed.

The four friends lowered the man on the mat into the room.

Jesus looked up at the faithful, waiting friends. He looked down at the paralyzed man. "Your sins are forgiven," he said.

Some people in the crowd whispered angrily, "Only GOD can forgive sins."

"Which is easier, forgiving or healing?" Jesus asked them. "I will do both!" Turning to the man on the mat, Jesus commanded, "Get up and WALK! Your legs are HEALED!"

The man JUMPED up from the mat. "Hooray!" shouted the four friends.

"AMAZING!" the crowd gasped. "Praise God! We've never seen anything like this!"

Wait, they made a hole in someone's ceiling?

It was for a good cause! Also, I'm sure they offered to pay for the damages.

Jesus Calms the Storm

MARK 4:35-41

FLASH! A bolt of lightning lit the sky. BOOM! Thunder echoed through the air. GASP! The frightened disciples huddled together in the middle of the boat.

? ?
How do wind and thunder sound?

"It's hard to see! There's too much rain!" Peter shouted.

"It's hard to hear! There's too much wind!" Philip yelled.

"Jesus!" John called out. "Help us!"

But Jesus didn't answer.

The disciples looked up, down, and all around. There! Jesus was sound asleep, lying in the back of the boat.

SPLASH! Big waves rocked the boat, but Jesus' eyes stayed closed. His breath was quiet and steady.

They hurried to Jesus and shook him awake. "Jesus," they cried, "WAKE UP! Don't you see that we are in danger?"

I don't like it when people wake me up from a nap.

But this was a boat emergency!

Jesus' eyes popped open. He saw the disciples' frightened faces. He felt the pouring rain. He heard the blowing wind and booming thunder.

Standing up, Jesus raised his arms toward the storm and commanded, "Peace! Be still!"

The wind heard and stopped blowing. The waves listened and stopped splashing. The rain obeyed and stopped pouring.

Jesus turned to the disciples. "Why were you afraid?" he asked. "Have FAITH! Trust in me. I will ALWAYS take care of you."

A breeze blew quietly across the water. The boat bobbed softly up and down. Everything was quiet. But the disciples' hearts pounded loudly with excitement. They were amazed by Jesus' power!

Filled with wonder, they whispered to one another, "Only GOD commands the wind and the sea! Who is JESUS, if the storm obeys HIM too?"

Of course Jesus wasn't scared of a storm. He can walk on water!

Who's the Greatest?

MARK 9:30-37

The disciples felt proud.

Jesus chose THEM to be his followers. Jesus taught THEM about God. They must be Jesus' FAVORITE people.

Many people followed Jesus. Many people listened to Jesus' teachings. But the disciples believed they were the BEST followers and the BEST listeners.

One day, as they were walking to a city named Capernaum, the disciples started arguing.

? ?

What do you argue about?

I wonder what the disciples argued about.

Most of my arguments are about kickball rules.

"I'm the GREATEST disciple," Peter said. "Jesus called me FIRST to follow him."

"No, I'm the greatest!" shouted John. "I ALWAYS listen to what Jesus says."

"You're both wrong," replied James. "I'M the greatest. I helped a man who was hurt!"

When they stopped at a house in Capernaum, Jesus asked them, "What were you arguing about?"

The disciples looked down. They shuffled their feet. None of them replied to Jesus.

Jesus frowned. "Don't you understand yet?" he asked them. "If you want to be FIRST, you have to come LAST. If you want to be the GREATEST, you have to SERVE everyone. Think of a child. In the emperor's eyes, a child is not important. But in God's eyes, a child is the MOST important. When you welcome a child, you welcome ME and GOD."

The disciples were very quiet. After all this time, they still had a lot to learn.

Well, that's good news. I'm last a lot.

Otto, that's because you're late. I think Jesus meant something different.

Jesus Blesses the Children

MARK 10:13-16

The disciples were trying to listen to Jesus, but they couldn't hear him. There were so many children laughing and talking. Small children, tall children, some walking, some crawling. Children were everywhere!

"Jesus!" one parent called out. "Please bless my child!"

"My daughter is sick," another said. "Lay your hands on her. Please heal her!"

The disciples pushed closer to Jesus. They shouted at the parents, "Take your children away! Jesus is trying to teach adults. He's too busy to talk with children!"

The disciples may have had a point. Sometimes kids can be very loud!

You'd know all about that, Otto.

"STOP," Jesus commanded. The disciples stopped shouting. The parents stopped calling out to Jesus. The children stopped laughing and talking.

Everyone turned to look at Jesus.

"Let the children come to me," Jesus said. "Do not stop them."

The children rushed to Jesus' side. A little girl crawled into his lap. A little boy jumped on his back. Other kids grabbed his hands. Jesus smiled.

Jesus spoke to the crowd. "Children are important to God. In God's kingdom, it's better to be like a kid! God's kingdom is about loving and sharing. Children love and share with ALL people. YOU can learn from a child how to be part of God's kingdom."

Jesus laid his hands on the children, hugged them, and blessed them.

? ?

Who hugs you?

It's like I always say: "Being a kid is great!"

More adults should try it.

A Camel through a Needle

MARK 10:17-31

A man ran up to Jesus.

"Teacher," the man panted. "I want to live with God FOREVER! How can I be part of God's kingdom?"

"You know God's rules," Jesus reminded him. "Don't kill anybody. Don't take things that aren't yours. Don't lie. Honor your father and mother."

The man was excited. "I've followed those rules since I was a kid!"

Jesus looked at the man and loved him. "You must do something else too," Jesus said. "Sell EVERYTHING you have and give the money to the poor. Then come and follow me."

The man hung his head and walked away. He didn't want to sell his things.

? ?

Which of your things would be hard to give away?

I bet I could give up everything to follow Jesus. As long as I got to keep my baseball cards . . . and my TV . . . and my bike . . . and my—

Everything means everything, Otto.

The disciples were surprised. "Sell EVERYTHING?" they asked.

Jesus explained, "It's easier for a CAMEL to fit through the EYE OF A NEEDLE than for people to enter God's kingdom if they love their possessions and their money. You have to love GOD more than you love your THINGS."

"If we do all those things, will we live with God forever?" wondered the disciples.

"It's not about what YOU do. It's about GOD," Jesus replied. "YOU aren't in charge of who enters God's kingdom. GOD is in charge. And with God, ALL things are possible. With God, the first will be last, and the last will be first."

What if it was a very small camel and a very big needle?

I don't think they make needles that big.

Bartimaeus Sees

MARK 10:46-52

Coins clinked. Donkeys brayed. Friends shouted out across the street. Bartimaeus was blind, but he knew the sounds of Jericho well. Suddenly, the racket hushed. Bartimaeus heard footsteps coming close.

? ?

What sounds do you hear?

A voice whispered, "Look! It's Jesus!"

"Jesus can heal the sick," thought Bartimaeus. "Jesus can return sight to people who are blind! Maybe Jesus could heal MY eyes!

"How can I get his attention?" he wondered.

Bartimaeus waved his arms. "Jesus! Have mercy on me!" he called.

A woman hushed him. "Bartimaeus, be QUIET!"

I like Bartimaeus's plan to get Jesus' attention.

Just yell and wave? Yes, I find that usually works.

Bartimaeus ignored the woman. He waved his arms faster and shouted louder. "JESUS! Over here! Please HELP me! Have mercy on me!"

Jesus heard his name. He turned to look. "Who's calling me?" he asked.

"It's just blind Bartimaeus. Don't pay attention to him," a man said.

Jesus didn't listen. "Bartimaeus, I hear you. What do you want me to do for you?"

Bartimaeus sprang to his feet. He rushed to Jesus. "Jesus, please heal my eyes so I can see. I BELIEVE you can!"

Jesus smiled. "Because you BELIEVED, you can SEE. Your FAITH has made you well."

Bartimaeus blinked his eyes. He SAW the coins that clinked. He SAW the donkeys that brayed. He SAW the silent crowd. He SAW Jesus smiling.

Bartimaeus left Jericho and followed Jesus, loudly praising God all the way.

Everything would look so amazing if you suddenly regained your sight!

Except for my room. It looks like dirty laundry exploded everywhere . . .

The Widow's Offering

MARK 12:41-44

Jesus pointed across the temple. "See that man by the treasury?" he asked.

The disciples saw him. The man strutted around and swished his fancy robes. This rich man looked pleased with himself.

Then he pulled a big bag of coins out of his robe. He looked around to make sure people were watching. "I am sharing MY MONEY!" he announced in a loud voice.

He dumped a handful of coins in the offering box. Jingle, jangle, CRASH! The coins dropped noisily into the box. Everyone looked. The man beamed. He looked VERY pleased with himself.

Just because someone is loud doesn't mean he deserves your attention.

Jesus pointed again. "See that widow over by the treasury?"

The disciples looked. Where was she?

? ?

Do you see the woman?

Then they saw her. A small woman in plain robes slipped between people to get to the offering box.

The widow dropped two small coins in the offering box. Clink, clink! Then she slipped away.

"Did you see the difference?" asked Jesus. "The rich man gave a LITTLE handful of his LARGE bag of money. He wanted EVERYONE to see him. The widow gave ALL her money—TWO coins. She didn't want to be seen. When you share, be like the widow. Give quietly. Don't try to impress others. THAT'S the kind of sharing I like to see."

So giving a little bit is more than giving a lot? I'm confused.

I think Jesus meant that the widow's gift meant a lot more because she gave all she had.

248

The Transfiguration

LUKE 9:28-36

Jesus and three disciples—Peter, James, and John—hiked up a mountain to pray.

As they prayed, Jesus CHANGED! His face and clothes became dazzling white.

"What's happening?" whispered James.

Peter squinted. "I can't look. It's too bright!"

"You HAVE to look," John insisted. "MOSES and ELIJAH just appeared!"

Moses and Elijah were two prophets from LONG ago. They talked with Jesus about things that would happen soon.

Peter, James, and John were tired from their hike. But they couldn't look away. They knew a visit from Moses and Elijah was IMPORTANT.

First rule of being a disciple: Follow Jesus. You never know who you might meet!

Peter shouted, "Jesus! It's GOOD to be here. Let's STAY! We will build houses for you and Moses and Elijah." James and John nodded.

? ?
Where's a place that you like to stay?

Suddenly a cloud covered the mountain. Everything was quiet.

Then a VOICE came from the cloud, "This is my Son! LISTEN to him." The disciples' mouths dropped open. They had heard GOD'S voice!

The cloud faded away. Moses and Elijah were nowhere to be seen. Jesus looked like himself again.

Jesus started walking down the mountain. Slowly, the disciples followed.

"I don't want to leave this mountain," James sighed. "I want to talk with Moses and Elijah."

"I want to STAY," John agreed, "and hear God's voice again!"

"Something AMAZING happened here," Peter said. "Something we will NEVER forget."

I've been surprised by things I've seen on hikes, but nothing as cool as that!

Best. Hike. Ever.

The Good Samaritan

"Help!" a Jewish man shouted from a ditch beside the road to Jericho. "Someone, help! I've been robbed!"

The man lay on the ground, hurt and afraid. He was a long way from home.

CRUNCH, CRUNCH. "What's that?" he wondered. The man lifted his head to see a priest walking toward him. Certainly this temple leader would help him. But the priest hurried away, pretending not to see him.

"Wait," the man whimpered, "don't go."

Just then, he heard footsteps from the OTHER direction. Turning his head, he spotted the dark robes of a Levite, someone who knew God's laws. "PLEASE help me!" the hurt man yelled. The Levite shook his head and RAN away.

"Will ANYONE help me?" the hurt man gasped. He closed his eyes and began to cry.

? ?

How do NEIGHBORS help each other?

254

Mom says I'm not allowed to talk to strangers.

But we can tell a trusted adult if we see someone who needs help.

STOMP, STOMP! The man's eyes flew open at the sound. A donkey stared down at him! Beside the donkey, the face of a Samaritan man appeared.

The Jewish man shook in fear. Jewish people and Samaritans did NOT like each other. Would this man hurt him too?

The Samaritan cleaned and bandaged the man's wounds, then gently lifted the injured man onto his donkey and started down the dusty road.

KNOCK, KNOCK! The Samaritan rapped on the door of the first inn they found. "This man is injured," he told the innkeeper. "Let him stay here until he is well. I will pay for EVERYTHING." The injured man's eyes opened wide with surprise. The Samaritan helped him inside and left.

"WHO was that?" asked the innkeeper.

The hurt man whispered, "He is my NEIGHBOR."

So the Samaritan came to the rescue? Just like a superhero!

Everything is like a superhero to you, Otto. But you're right.

Mary and Martha

LUKE 10:38-42

"Cook the food. They'll be hungry. Shake the rug. No more dust. Light the lamps. The sun is setting."

Martha was busy getting ready for Jesus to visit.

"Why isn't my sister, Mary, helping me?" grumbled Martha.

Mary was sitting alone. She was getting ready for Jesus to visit too.

"I have so many questions to ask Jesus," she thought. "What is God really like? How many people have you healed? Where will you teach next?"

? ?

What questions would you like to ask Jesus?

Knock, knock. Martha rushed to the door. Mary skipped right behind her. "Jesus is HERE!" they exclaimed together.

Jesus and twelve disciples stood at the door. Mary and Martha welcomed Jesus. "Come in," said the sisters. "We've been waiting for you."

Cooking for 13 visitors is a lot of work!

Don't they have a butler for things like that?

After washing their feet, the guests sat down. Peter sat near the door. James sat by the window. Mary sat right in FRONT of Jesus. Her ears were ready to listen.

Martha hurried to check the food. She straightened the rug. She lit another lamp.

"WHAT is Mary DOING?" she wondered.

Martha looked around. She saw Peter sitting near the door. She saw James sitting by the window. She saw Mary sitting right in FRONT of Jesus.

Martha marched over to Jesus. "I worked ALL day, with NO help, to get ready for your visit," she said in her most frustrated voice. "Tell Mary to get up and HELP me!"

Jesus touched Martha's arm and smiled. "Martha. You are so busy. Preparing for a guest is important, but listening is MORE important. Mary understands this. I won't tell her to stop."

Why did they wash their feet? Were they going to eat with them?

Their feet were dirty. People wore sandals a lot more back then.

The Lost Sheep and Lost Coin

LUKE 15:1-10

"Jesus is welcoming too many outcast people," grumbled the Pharisees. "Even tax collectors, people who are sick, and people who ALWAYS mess up."

"You don't understand," Jesus told the Pharisees. "ALL people need to learn about God. Listen," he said.

A shepherd had 100 sheep. ONE wandered away from the flock. He left the 99 to look for the ONE that was lost!

? ?
What have you lost?

He looked behind the bushes. It wasn't there!
He looked near the pond. It wasn't there!
He looked over the hill. It wasn't there!
He looked EVERYWHERE until . . . he FOUND it!
The shepherd shared his good news with his friends and neighbors. Everyone CHEERED! The shepherd FOUND his ONE lost sheep!

"Why is ONE lost thing so important?" wondered the Pharisees.

The shepherd kept track of 100 sheep! I had trouble caring for our one class hamster over Christmas break.

Jesus told them another story.

A woman had ten silver coins. She lost ONE.

The woman lit a lamp and looked for the ONE that was lost!

She looked on top of the cupboard. It wasn't there!

She looked under the rug. It wasn't there!

She looked inside the jar. It wasn't there!

She looked EVERYWHERE until . . . she FOUND it!

The woman shared her good news with her friends and neighbors. Everyone CHEERED! The woman FOUND her ONE lost coin!

"In the same way," Jesus told the Pharisees, "God and all the angels CHEER when ONE lost person is FOUND!"

Wait, wait, wait! Where did she find the coin?

In the last place she looked. That's usually where lost things are.

The Prodigal Son

LUKE 15:11-32

"Oink!" squealed the pigs. The man sighed. He was SO hungry. He had NO money, NO food, and NO bed to sleep in. The pigs slurped their slop. "They're full while I'm hungry," he groaned. His stomach growled.

The man missed his father. He wished he hadn't left home and wasted ALL the money his father gave him. Food and drinks! Parties! Fancy clothes! Now his inheritance was GONE.

SPLAT! A pig lay down next to him, smearing his robes with mud.

"I want to go HOME!" the man cried. "I don't deserve to be my father's son. I will ask to be his servant."

He shouldn't be right next to the pigs if he doesn't want to get dirty.

It sounds like he's made lots of bad choices before that, Otto.

The man walked toward home, leaving a trail of muddy footprints. In the distance he saw a tiny dot. "My father's house!" he thought.

The man's father spotted him. "My son!" the father cried. He ran to meet his son.

The man hung his head. "Father, I'm sorry," he said. "I am not worthy to be your son."

The father hugged his son. "You will ALWAYS be my son!" He grinned. "And now you're HOME. Let's CELEBRATE!"

? ?

How does your family celebrate?

The man's brother was angry. "He left HOME!" the brother yelled. "He wasted all YOUR money! I STAYED and worked hard EVERY DAY! Father, why are you happy to see him?"

"You are my son, and I love you," the father answered. "I thought I'd never see your brother again. He was lost but now is FOUND!"

So . . . God is like a parent who loves us, even when we mess up and make mistakes?

You're really starting to get these parables, Otto.

Jesus Heals Ten

LUKE 17:11-19

Jesus was walking to Jerusalem. "Jesus! JESUS!" He heard ten voices calling his name. Jesus looked around. Where were they?

In the distance, Jesus saw ten people with leprosy limping toward him. Their skin was bright red and bumpy. Some were missing fingers. And toes!

"Jesus, help us!" one man called out.

"Our skin hurts," a woman cried.

"We haven't seen our families in years," an older man said.

"Please," another woman begged, "I have FAITH you can HEAL us!"

Everyone stayed away from people with leprosy. They were afraid they would catch it too. But Jesus wasn't afraid.

Mosquito bites make my skin red and bumpy.

Leprosy is more serious. It's an infection.

"Go and show yourselves to the priests," Jesus told them.

Ten people rushed to see the priests. One of them stopped in his tracks. "WAIT!" he yelled. He looked at his friends. Their skin was SMOOTH. The red bumps were GONE. He looked at his hands and feet. TEN fingers! TEN toes! "We're HEALED!" he shouted.

The man raced back and skidded to a halt in front of Jesus. He fell to the ground. "Praise GOD! I'm HEALED!" he exclaimed. "Thank you, JESUS! You made me well again!"

Jesus looked around. "Weren't there ten of you?" he asked, puzzled. "NINE aren't here. Did they forget to thank God for healing them?

? ?
When have you forgotten to say thank you?

"Get up!" Jesus said. "It's time to go home. I healed you because you had FAITH!"

How could they forget to say thank you?

Maybe they were too excited to see their families again.

Zacchaeus

LUKE 19:1-10

Zacchaeus jumped UP and DOWN, trying to see.

"I want to see Jesus!" he shouted. But the crowd wouldn't let him see.

"I know who ZACCHAEUS is," one neighbor grumbled. "He's that tax collector who STEALS from us."

Zacchaeus stomped his foot. He REALLY wanted to see Jesus. So little Zacchaeus climbed UP a big tree.

? ?

What does it feel like when you're too little for something?

Zacchaeus looked UP and DOWN the street. "Where's Jesus?" he wondered.

"Hi, Zacchaeus!" a voice said.

Zacchaeus looked DOWN to see who it was. JESUS looked UP at Zacchaeus!

If he was too short, why didn't he just activate his jet boots?

You're the only one I know who has jet boots, Leo.

"Jesus, you don't want to talk to HIM," a man said. "He steals and lies!"

Jesus heard the people grumbling about Zacchaeus.

"Come DOWN, Zacchaeus!" Jesus said. "Cheer UP! I'm staying at your house today."

What a surprise! Zacchaeus hurried DOWN the tree. He looked UP at Jesus. "You're welcome in my house!"

Zacchaeus wanted Jesus to love and forgive him. He wanted everyone to know that being with Jesus could change him.

"I'm sorry, Lord!" Zacchaeus cried. "I will give half of my things to the poor! I will pay back the money I've stolen. Times FOUR!"

"Zacchaeus, my friend," Jesus said. "God sent me to visit people just like YOU! You asked for forgiveness, and God forgives you!"

If Jesus wanted to stay at my house, I'd let him stay in the nicest guest room.

How many guest rooms do you have, Ruby?

About 30. Why, is that a lot?

Water into Wine

JOHN 2:1-11

Jesus, his disciples, and his mother, Mary, were attending a wedding in Cana. All the guests were talking and eating, laughing and celebrating. Mary watched the beautiful bride and handsome groom dance together.

Drip, drip, drip. Mary watched the servants pour the last drops of wine.

? ?
What happens if you run out of something at a party?

"Jesus," she whispered. "They are out of wine. DO something!"

"Mother," Jesus whispered back, "that is not my concern."

But Mary knew Jesus could help. She waved over the servants. "Do whatever Jesus tells you."

You should always make sure you have everything ready for your party before it starts. That's just good hosting!

Jesus looked around. He saw six huge stone jars for hand washing standing empty.

"Fill those jars with clean water," Jesus told the servants. So the servants filled EVERY jar to the tip top with water. A LOT of water. But they wondered what to do next.

"Fill your pitcher from those jars," Jesus said. "Take it to the chief steward."

The servants filled the pitcher and brought it to the steward. He filled his glass from the pitcher. Not with WATER. But with WINE! All six jars were filled with wine. A LOT of wine.

"AMAZING!" said the chief steward to the groom. "This is the best wine I've ever tasted! Now the celebration can continue!"

Changing water to wine was the first of many amazing things Jesus did.

Jesus totally saved that wedding!

I've said it before, and I'll say it again. Jesus is awesome.

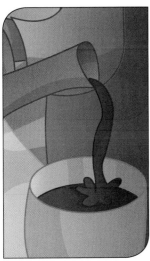

Nicodemus

JOHN 3:1-17

Tiptoe . . . tiptoe . . . tiptoe. Nicodemus the Pharisee crept out at night to meet Jesus.

Pharisees such as Nicodemus carefully studied God's laws and tried to keep all the rules. Jesus frustrated the Pharisees because he taught about God's LOVE first, not God's LAWS. Nicodemus liked Jesus.

"Psst! Jesus! Over here!" Nicodemus called Jesus over into the shadows. "I know you're from God. You teach and heal people."

"Yes," Jesus replied, "but to really know God, you have to be born again from above."

"What?" Nicodemus whispered. "You can only be born once! You can't have two birthdays!"

Jesus answered firmly, "You're born once as a baby. But you can be born again as a child of God!"

A Pharisee who is nice to Jesus? You don't see many of those in these stories!

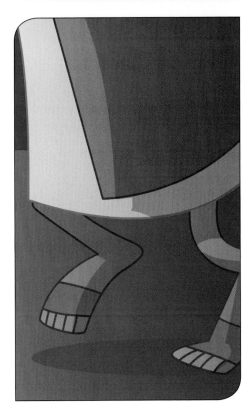

"Shhh!" Nicodemus urged. He didn't want the other Pharisees to know he was talking with Jesus.

? ?
Where do you go to be alone with Jesus?

"You teach about God! You should understand," Jesus went on. "Anyone who believes in me will be born again and will have new life."

Nicodemus thought hard, stroking his beard. "Born again . . . new life . . . I don't understand!"

"I'll say it clearly," Jesus said. "God LOVES the world—so God sent his Son. Whoever believes in the Son will not die, but will have eternal life with God. I'm not here to punish the world. I'm here to save it!"

Why can't Nicodemus understand what Jesus is talking about?

This is a lot of new information for Nicodemus. No one had ever talked about these things before.

The Woman at the Well

JOHN 4:5-30

Jesus kicked the dust from his sandals. He plopped down on the edge of a well in Samaria.

A Samaritan woman lowered her bucket down, down, down into the well. Then she pulled it up, up, up, filled with water. She poured the water into a jar.

Jesus shielded his eyes from the hot sun. "Please give me a drink," he said to the woman.

The woman jumped and gasped in surprise. Jewish people didn't talk to Samaritans! Jewish people didn't LIKE Samaritans.

"Why would YOU ask ME for water?" she asked. "I'm a Samaritan."

"It's very hot, and I've walked a LONG way. I'm thirsty," Jesus replied.

Of course Jesus is going to like her. Jesus likes everyone!

It doesn't sound like she knows that yet.

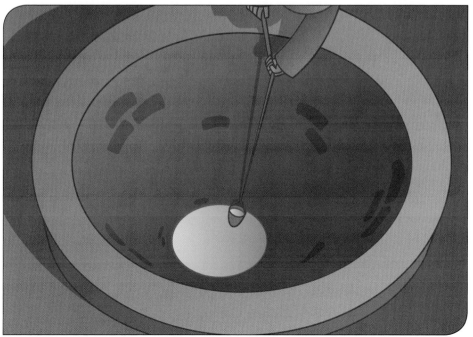

Jesus touched the jar full of water. "This water is good for the body. But I can give you LIVING water. Water that will fill you up with God's LOVE! You will never be thirsty again."

"But you don't even have a bucket," the woman replied. "How are you going to get it?"

"I AM the living water," Jesus said.

Jesus told the woman all he knew about her. He told her details she didn't expect a stranger to know.

? ?

Who knows all about you?

"I don't understand how you know these things," she said. "But I do know the Messiah is coming."

"That's me!" Jesus exclaimed. "I am the Messiah!"

The woman's eyes grew wide with amazement. She raced to tell the people in her town. Running through the streets, she shouted, "Come and see!"

Many people followed the woman to meet Jesus.

She gives him water and Jesus gives her God's love? That's a pretty good deal.

I'd take that deal.

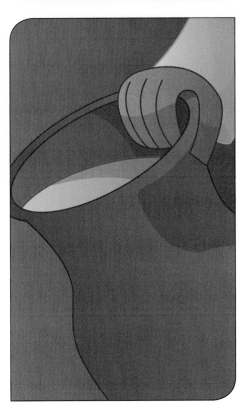

Jesus Feeds 5,000

JOHN 6:1-21

"Don't forget your lunch," a mother told her son.

The boy looked inside his basket. "One, two, three, four, five," he counted. "FIVE small barley loaves. One, two. And TWO fish!"

The boy swung his basket as he scurried on his way. "How many people will come to hear Jesus today?" he wondered.

A HUGE crowd of people gathered by the sea to hear Jesus. The boy wiggled and squeezed his way to the front to hear what Jesus was saying.

"Where can we buy bread for all of these people to eat?" Jesus asked Philip. "They must be hungry."

Philip's eyes grew big. "ALL of them? There must be 5,000 people here!" he responded. "We don't have enough money to buy bread for EVERYONE!"

? ?

What kind of food might you feed 5,000 people?

The boy held up his basket. "I can share my lunch," he offered.

All the people there should have had their mothers pack them lunch too!

Adults usually have to make their own lunch. It's tough.

Andrew counted, "One, two, three, four, five. FIVE loaves! One, two. And TWO fish! How will this feed 5,000 people?"

Smiling, Jesus picked up the five loaves and two fish. "Thank you, Father, for this food," he prayed.

Jesus passed the boy's lunch to the crowd. Each person took plenty of bread and fish to eat. Everyone ate until they were full!

The disciples gathered the leftover food into baskets.

"One, two, three, four, five," the boy started to count the baskets.

A man wondered, "How did five loaves and two fish feed everyone?"

"Six, seven, eight, nine," the boy continued.

A woman gasped in surprise, "How can there be any leftovers?"

"Ten, eleven, TWELVE baskets of leftovers!" the boy finished counting. "It's a miracle!"

The boy and the whole crowd could not wait to tell everyone what Jesus had done!

All that bread and fish is pretty impressive. But I would have asked for pineapple pizza!

The Good Shepherd

JOHN 10:11-18

Jesus was the best kind of leader. He cared about his friends and disciples. He wanted them to feel safe and strong and loved.

? ?
Who's the best leader you know?

"I am the good shepherd," said Jesus. The disciples were confused. Jesus was a TEACHER of people, not a SHEPHERD of sheep.

Jesus saw the disciples' puzzled faces. "What does a good shepherd do?" Jesus asked.

"A good shepherd leads his sheep to food and water," Andrew said.

"He protects the sheep from dangerous wolves!" John added.

"He finds lost sheep and brings them back to the flock," Peter answered.

 Do you think Jesus meant people are like sheep or sheep are like people?

Yes.

"I do ALL these things for YOU," Jesus said. "I lead you to the love of God. I protect you from harm. When you lose your way, I find you. I am the good shepherd."

The disciples nodded. Jesus cared for them, just like a good shepherd cares for his sheep.

Jesus knew each of his disciples very well, like a good shepherd knows the sound and face of each of his sheep.

Jesus looked at his disciples with love in his eyes. "The best shepherds love their sheep," he said. "I am the kind of shepherd who loves you enough to die for you. This is what I have learned from my Father."

Do you think Jesus would know me if I made this face?

Yes, Jesus knows you even when you're being weird.

Jesus Raises Lazarus

JOHN 11:1-45

The disciples had never seen Jesus cry. But he was crying now.

? ?
When have you seen a grown-up cry?

Jesus put his arm around Mary. Her face was wet with tears.

Mary and Martha's brother Lazarus, a good friend of Jesus, had died.

When Jesus heard Lazarus was sick, he was in another town far away. Jesus waited two days before traveling to Bethany to see his friend. By the time Jesus and the disciples arrived, Lazarus had died.

"If you had been here," Mary cried, "Lazarus would not have died."

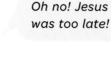

Oh no! Jesus was too late!

Give it time, Otto. I'm sure Jesus has a plan.

"Your brother Lazarus will rise again," Jesus assured Mary. Mary wiped her tears.

Jesus, Mary, and her sister Martha went to the tomb. Friends and neighbors gathered around the tomb to grieve with Mary and Martha.

"Remove the stone," Jesus said. The crowd shoved aside the huge stone blocking the tomb.

Martha whispered, "But, Jesus, Lazarus has already been dead for four days!"

Jesus turned his eyes to God and prayed, "Father, thank you for always hearing me. Help this crowd see what's about to happen and BELIEVE!"

"LAZARUS!" Jesus shouted. "COME OUT!"

The crowd GASPED. It was Lazarus! WALKING out of the tomb! Lazarus was ALIVE again!

Many people who saw this believed in God.

How could anyone see that and not believe in God? Jesus just brought someone back to life! From the dead!

Mary Anoints Jesus

JOHN 12:1-8

Lazarus, Martha, and the disciples stopped eating and stared. They couldn't believe their eyes— or their noses. Mary was anointing Jesus' FEET. With PERFUME. EXPENSIVE perfume.

Jesus and his disciples were visiting the home of Lazarus, the man Jesus raised from death. Lazarus's sisters, Mary and Martha, had served them dinner.

The disciples sniffed. The room was filled with the strong smell of perfume.

Mary lowered her head. She wiped the dripping perfume from Jesus' sandy feet. With her HAIR.

They disciples looked at each other. Some were confused. Others were surprised. Judas's face was bright red. He was ANGRY.

Why is Judas so angry?

Maybe he has a sensitive nose.

Judas jumped up. "WHY are you wasting that EXPENSIVE perfume?" he demanded. "You could have SOLD it. You could have bought FOOD for HUNDREDS of hungry people!"

Mary continued wiping Jesus' feet. Jesus looked right at Judas. "Leave her ALONE."

Judas couldn't believe it. WHY did Jesus defend Mary?

"You will always be able to help hungry people," Jesus continued. "But you won't always be able to show love for me. Mary understands. I am walking into danger in Jerusalem. This might be her last chance to do something kind for me."

? ?

What's something kind you could do for someone?

They could have fed hundreds of people by selling that perfume? It must have smelled amazing!

Jesus the Vine

JOHN 15:1-17

Jesus knew he wouldn't be able to stay with his disciples forever. He wanted them to understand how much he loved them.

"God's family is like a vine full of grapes," Jesus said.

The disciples raised their eyebrows. What did love have to do with vines of grapes?

"What happens when a branch is cut from the vine?" Jesus asked.

"The branch can't grow," answered James.

"When a branch is cut from the vine, it can't grow fruit. But what happens when branches are attached to the vine?"

"They grow lots of grapes!" Peter said.

Jesus nodded. "I am the vine. You are the branches. I love you so you can love others."

? ?
How do you show love to people?

So remember,
share your love
with others,
and don't chop
up grape vines.

Jesus looked at his disciples with love. "You are my friends. I love you so much that I am willing to give up my life for you. That is the greatest love you can have for someone."

The disciples were amazed. Jesus would give up EVERYTHING. For THEM!

"This is my commandment: Love each other like I love YOU," Jesus said.

"Jesus ALWAYS loves us—no matter what," the disciples thought. "Jesus is willing to give up his LIFE for us. How can we love each other like THAT?"

Jesus smiled at his friends. "Love each other. Be joyful. Go and grow fruit. Go and love others so they know God's love!"

That's a tall order. Jesus made loving everyone look easy.

Loving all of us is Jesus' thing!

Jesus Enters Jerusalem

MATTHEW 21:1-11   **LUKE 19:28-40**

Jerusalem was overflowing with people celebrating the Passover festival. Jesus waited to enter the town. He asked two disciples to bring him a young donkey.

"HOSANNA! HOSANNA!" the crowd in Jerusalem cheered. Jesus rode the donkey through the crowds. The people tossed coats and palm branches on the road to welcome him.

? ?

How do you celebrate Palm Sunday?

"Jesus! Over here!" a little boy shouted joyfully.

The boy's sister waved a palm branch in the air. "Hooray! It's Jesus!"

In the distance, religious leaders frowned. They worried about the cheering. And the shouting. And the waving. "What is Jesus DOING?" they grumbled. "All this NOISE could get us in trouble with the Romans."

Those leaders sound grumpy for no reason.

Yeah, who doesn't like waving palm branches?

The people were excited and pressed in to see Jesus. They sang songs and shouted praises.

"Blessed is Jesus! He comes in God's name!"

"Hosanna in the highest heaven!"

"Our king has come! Hooray!"

"HOSANNA!"

The religious leaders glared. The crowd was TOO BIG. There were TOO MANY people. They were TOO EXCITED. "We can't let this get out of control," they thought.

One of the leaders ran up to Jesus and shouted, "Hey! Tell this crowd to BE QUIET!"

Jesus looked down at the man. "Even if every PERSON was quiet," Jesus said, "the STONES would shout out."

The leader didn't know what Jesus was talking about. Frustrated, he stomped away through the cheering crowd.

I think I'd rather hear a bunch of excited people shouting than a bunch of stones. Shouting stones would be weird.

The Last Supper

MATTHEW 26:14-29   LUKE 22:14-23

"And THEN," said Peter, "God told Moses to part the sea, and all the Israelites crossed on DRY LAND. They were SAFE! They were FREE!"

The disciples and Jesus were celebrating the Passover feast together. The table was filled with food. They shared lamb and unleavened bread. They remembered the story of how God freed the Israelites from slavery.

While they ate, Jesus picked up a loaf of bread. He blessed the loaf and broke it in half. The disciples passed the loaf around the table. Everyone tore off a piece to eat.

"Take this bread and eat it," said Jesus. "This is my body. Whenever you eat this bread, remember me."

I'm confused. If Jesus is right there, why would he ask the disciples to remember him?

I think he's talking about when he won't be right there with them anymore.

Jesus poured a cup of wine and thanked God for it. The disciples passed the cup around the table. Everyone took a drink from the cup.

"Take this wine and drink," Jesus said. "This is my blood poured out for the forgiveness of sins. Whenever you drink this wine, remember me."

? ?

How does your church celebrate communion?

"Jesus, of course we'll always remember you," said Matthew. "But where are you going?"

Jesus looked at each of his friends. "I am glad to eat this meal with you. But soon I will have to leave you. Someday we will share a meal again. It will be on a great day when everyone joins together to praise God."

Bread and body? Wine and blood? Those words sound very familiar.

During communion, we do what Jesus taught the disciples to do. It started with this meal.

Jesus Is Betrayed

MARK 14:26-50

Jesus looked at each of his disciples. "You will all desert me," he said.

Matthew looked at Peter. Peter looked at James. James turned to look at Judas. But Judas wasn't there. Where did Judas go?

Everybody looked at Jesus. "I would never desert you!" Peter said.

"Yes, you will," Jesus sighed.

Jesus led the disciples to a garden called Gethsemane. The disciples sat on the soft grass in the dark night. They felt drowsy.

"Stay here," Jesus said to them. "I am going to pray. Stay awake while I'm gone. Wait for me."

? ?

Where do you pray?

Staying awake and waiting sounds easy. Now that Jesus told them, all they have to do is not desert him.

I don't think anything was easy for the disciples then, Otto.

Jesus walked farther into the garden. He fell to the ground. "Father," Jesus prayed, "if it is possible, please don't let me suffer. But I will do what must be done."

When Jesus returned, all the disciples were asleep.

Jesus shook them awake. "Couldn't you stay awake with me?"

Just then Judas and a crowd of soldiers arrived in the garden.

Judas whispered his plan to the soldiers. "I will kiss the one you want." He walked up to Jesus and kissed him.

The soldiers arrested Jesus. The disciples gasped in fear. Jesus was in trouble! What if soldiers arrested them too? They ran away from the garden. Jesus' disciples all deserted him.

What? They just said they wouldn't desert him! They have terrible memories!

Sometimes it's hard to stand up for your friends, even when you say you'll do it.

Jesus Is Crucified

LUKE 23:26-56

Three crosses stood on a hill. Jesus' cross was in the middle. Two criminals were crucified with him—one on his right and one on his left.

There were nails in Jesus' hands and feet, holding him to the cross. He wore a crown like a king. But it was made of thorns.

? ?

When you touch a thorn, how does it feel?

The soldiers and religious leaders laughed and shouted cruel things at Jesus.

"Hail the king of the Jews!"

"He's not such a king now!"

"If you're the Son of God, SAVE yourself!"

Jesus prayed, "Father, forgive them. They don't know what they are doing."

Jesus' friends and family knelt by the cross. They cried and prayed.

Jesus forgave the people who were putting him to death? That's amazing.

Jesus forgives everyone.

One criminal mocked Jesus. "If you are the Messiah, save yourself AND us!"

But the criminal on the other side said, "This man, Jesus, has done NOTHING wrong." He then said to Jesus, "When you come into your kingdom, remember me."

"I will always remember you," Jesus said. "You are with me today and forever."

Jesus prayed to God. His voice was weak and quiet and tired. "Father, into your hands I give my spirit."

Then Jesus breathed his last breath and died.

There's more to the story, right? That would be the saddest story ever if that was the end.

There's more.

Jesus Is Risen

MATTHEW 28:1-10　　**JOHN 20:1-18**

Sunday morning. The sun peeked over the trees.
The sky was filled with pink and orange light.

As soon as Mary Magdalene and her friends woke
up, they remembered what had happened two days
before. Jesus died on a cross. They wiped tears from
their eyes. They missed Jesus very much. But now it
was time to anoint Jesus' body.

The women walked quietly to the tomb that held
Jesus' body. When they arrived, the ground began to
shake beneath their feet. An earthquake! Mary and
the other women were afraid. They held tightly to
each other.

Everything became still. The women slowly
stepped closer to the tomb. The huge stone was
GONE! Someone had rolled it away!

The women looked into the tomb and gasped!
Jesus' body was GONE!

*I wonder what
anointing means.*

That's when they put spices on the bodies of people who died.

The women blinked their eyes. "Who's that?" they wondered. An angel! Dressed in dazzling white!

"Don't be afraid," the angel said. "You are looking for Jesus, but he isn't here. Jesus is alive! GO and TELL his disciples. Jesus is RISEN!"

"Could it be true?" the women wondered.

Mary and her friends rushed to tell the other disciples. Suddenly, Jesus appeared.

"Greetings," he said. The women reached out to touch him.

"Jesus! It's you!" Mary exclaimed.

Her friends jumped and clapped their hands.

? ?
When do you jump and clap your hands?

Jesus smiled at them. "GO and TELL my disciples. I'm alive!"

The women raced down the road to share the good news. Jesus is RISEN!

Wow! Jesus is risen! How did that HAPPEN?

No one is quite sure of the logistics, Ada.

On the Road to Emmaus

LUKE 24:13-35

"Do you think Jesus is really ALIVE?" Cleopas kicked a rock in the road.

"I don't know," his friend shrugged. The two men walked along the road to Emmaus.

? ?
Where do you like to walk?

Somebody joined them as they walked. "What are you talking about?" the stranger asked.

Cleopas sighed. "Are you the only person in Jerusalem who doesn't know about Jesus?"

"Who?" asked the man.

"Jesus of Nazareth. Our friend and teacher. He taught about God's LOVE and FORGIVENESS," Cleopas explained. "He healed people. The religious leaders didn't like him. So Jesus was killed on a cross."

I think I know who
the stranger is!

Moses? I'll bet it's Moses.

"But TODAY," Cleopas's friend interrupted, "some women went to Jesus' tomb. It was EMPTY. An angel told them Jesus is ALIVE. Is that possible?"

The stranger smiled. He taught them what the scriptures said about God's Messiah.

The three men walked together. They talked about Jesus the WHOLE way.

It was dark when they reached Emmaus. "Please stay and eat with us," Cleopas said to the man. At supper, the man BLESSED the bread and BROKE it.

Suddenly, Cleopas's eyes grew wide. He realized the man was JESUS!

Jesus smiled at them. Then he disappeared.

"Jesus was HERE!" Cleopas's heart pounded.

"He's ALIVE!" his friend shouted.

They jumped up from the table. They RACED back to Jerusalem that same night! They couldn't wait to tell the disciples they had seen JESUS!

They must have been in a hurry to run at night in the dark. I hope they brought a flashlight.

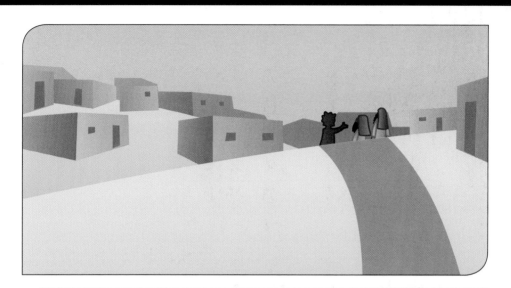

Thomas Wonders

JOHN 20:19-31

SLAM went the door. CLICK went the lock.
No one coming in. No one going out.
Ten of Jesus' disciples were hiding in a house. One wasn't there—Thomas.

The disciples were afraid. Jesus died on a cross. Would they be killed, too?

Suddenly, Jesus appeared in the locked room with them! "Peace be with you," said Jesus.

The disciples stared. Their mouths dropped open. Could it REALLY be Jesus? Jesus smiled. He showed them his hands. They saw holes from the nails.

"JESUS! IT'S YOU!" the disciples shouted.

WHOOSH! Jesus breathed his Spirit on them. "GO! Tell everyone I'm alive! Take my Spirit with you."

? ?

Who can you tell about Jesus?

How could Jesus get in a locked room?

Jesus came back from the dead and YOU'RE thinking about how he got into the room?

Ten disciples were ready to tell. But one disciple—Thomas—wasn't in the house that day. He didn't see or hear Jesus.

When the disciples saw Thomas, they shouted, "Jesus is ALIVE!"

"WHAT?" wondered Thomas. "I won't believe it until I see Jesus and touch his hands with my finger."

One week later, ALL of Jesus' disciples were back in the house, even Thomas.

Suddenly, Jesus appeared AGAIN!

"Peace be with you," he said. "Thomas, touch my hands. Believe!"

Thomas answered, "My Lord and my God!"

Jesus blesses everyone who has not seen him but still BELIEVES.

Does that blessing include people who believe today?

Yes! It includes EVERYONE who believes!

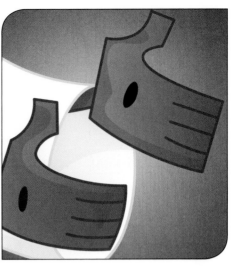

The Great Commission

MATTHEW 28:16-20

Eleven disciples waited excitedly to meet the risen Jesus. They peered down from a mountaintop in Galilee.

"Why did Jesus ask us here?" Philip wondered.

"Maybe," guessed Peter, "he's going to teach and heal again!"

"I hope we can still follow him," said John.

Just then, Jesus arrived. The disciples dropped to their knees.

"Jesus is alive!" they prayed. "Thank you, God!"

Peter lifted up his head. "Jesus, are you going to teach and heal again?" he asked.

Jesus shook his head. "It's YOUR turn now. I taught you about God's love. I healed God's people. Now you must teach and heal in my name."

Now the disciples are going to teach and heal like Jesus? Those are some big shoes to fill!

They wore sandals, Leo. Obviously.

338

"But we CAN'T heal people like YOU do!" Peter protested. "We CAN'T teach about God the way YOU do!"

? ?

When have you been asked to do something you thought you couldn't do?

"Yes, you CAN," Jesus assured them. "YOU have been given the AUTHORITY to teach and heal God's people."

"We can HEAL people?" James asked, amazed.

Jesus smiled at his disciples. "You will be my APOSTLES. Go in MY name. Travel all over the world. Teach and heal people. Baptize them in the name of the Father, the Son, and the Holy Spirit."

The eleven looked at each other. Could they REALLY do those things?

"You won't be alone," Jesus added. "Remember, I'm ALWAYS with you. Now and forever."

So the apostles traveled the earth, doing good.

Kind of like superheroes!

Yeah, a lot like superheroes.

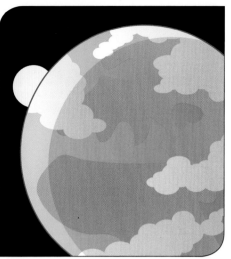

341

Jesus Ascends

ACTS 1:6-14

The disciples were amazed. First Jesus died. Then he rose from the dead.

They watched Jesus closely. He looked normal. Alive. Human!

Would he stay with them longer? Would he continue to teach and heal and perform miracles?

Peter quietly wondered, "Can Jesus stay with us forever now?"

"I don't think so," whispered John.

? ?

When do you whisper?

"But what will happen next?" asked Matthew.

"I can tell you what happens next," said Jesus.

You don't have to whisper around Jesus. Just ask him if you have a question. He's a teacher. He likes questions.

Jesus smiled at his friends. "You've been my disciples. And my friends! You've followed me, learned from me, and seen my healings and miracles."

The disciples nodded.

"But soon you will have a new calling," Jesus explained. "God's Spirit will be on you. You will tell others the story of everything that has happened to us."

"You mean tell people about God's love?" asked Matthew.

"And about the healings?" asked John.

"And the miracles too?" asked Peter.

"YES!" said Jesus. "Share ALL those stories. And tell about how I died and rose from the dead. Go all over the world. Tell EVERYONE about me so they will FOLLOW me!"

Suddenly, Jesus was lifted into the clouds. Up, up, up he went until the disciples couldn't see him anymore. They were shocked!

Another amazing story about Jesus to tell the people!

So the disciples told people, and those people told people, until the story finally came to us.

And now if we tell people, those people will tell even more people about Jesus!

The Holy Spirit at Pentecost

ACTS 2:1-21

A gust of wind BLASTED through the house in Jerusalem. The disciples jumped up from the table. Andrew grabbed the bread. John and James grabbed the cups. The tablecloth FLEW into the air. Plates CRASHED to the floor.

The disciples were celebrating the festival of Pentecost. But now their meal was a mess.

Andrew dropped the bread in surprise. A flame of fire floated over each disciple's head! The flames were bright red, orange, and yellow. But they weren't HOT!

Andrew pointed to the flames. "LOOK!"

The disciples looked. John and James dropped the cups. Peter's and Simon's eyes grew wide. Bartholomew's and Philip's mouths dropped open. Matthew, Thomas, and Matthias gasped. Thaddaeus and the other James pointed to Andrew's head. "You have a flame too!"

And that is why you should close the windows when you're eating dinner.

Suddenly the disciples began to speak in different languages. Latin, Greek, Arabic—ALL the languages of the WORLD! They rushed outside.

"We are filled with God's Spirit!" shouted Matthew.

"God is the ruler of all!" Philip exclaimed.

The street filled with Jewish people from many countries who were celebrating Pentecost in Jerusalem.

Every person, no matter where they had come from, heard the disciples speaking about God's power in their OWN LANGUAGE!

? ?

When do you hear different languages?

The people couldn't believe their EARS! Some in the crowd sneered. They could not believe that the disciples could actually speak all the languages. But many other people were amazed.

Peter yelled, "Each of you hears our words in your own language. God's Spirit has made this possible!"

So the disciples could suddenly speak all those different languages? I've never heard of that superpower before!

Early Believers Share

ACTS 4:32-35

The first Christians were believers who started forming church families. Men and women, boys and girls were all eager to learn about Jesus together.

"Jesus wants us to love each other," one believer said. "He said we should love others like God loves us." The people in the church family nodded. They worked hard to show love to everyone.

"What about SHARING?" a little boy asked.

"Jesus taught us to share EVERYTHING," said an older man. "He told his followers to share with people in need."

"What could WE share?" a woman asked.

The believers shared with each other. Now they looked for what they could share with people outside their church family.

The first churches didn't use the word Christian. They just called each other believers.

The little boy ran into the room holding a pair of sandals. "These are too small for me! We can share them with another boy!"

A young girl held out a small bundle. "We baked bread this morning. We can share with someone who is hungry."

A man laid a hammer and nails on a table. "We have tools for building. We can share with people who need to fix things."

? ?

Who do you know who shares?

The believers gave away all kinds of things. Clothing, food, and money, too! EVERY believer found something important to share inside and outside their church family.

> *I could share my food. And probably my video games. But does Jesus even want me to share my limited edition action figure collection?*

> *Yes, Otto. Jesus wants us to share everything. Even your limited edition action figure collection.*

Saul's Conversion

ACTS 9:1-20

Saul did NOT believe Jesus was the Messiah. He wanted everyone to STOP teaching about Jesus. Saul was traveling to Damascus to arrest believers and throw them in JAIL!

STOMP, STOMP, STOMP went Saul's feet. Then FLASH! A bright light from heaven knocked him to the ground!

"What was THAT?" yelled Saul.

Saul heard a voice rumble. "Saul, why are you against me? What are you doing?"

"Who are you?" Saul asked the voice.

The voice rumbled again. "I am JESUS. Go to Damascus. I will tell you what to do!"

Saul opened his eyes, but he couldn't see!

Now Saul was SCARED. "What's happening to me?" he wondered.

A blinding flash of light? Jesus sure knew how to get Saul's attention.

I would just yell, "Hey, Saul, listen up!"

Saul's friends helped him stand. They brushed dirt from his robes and led him to Damascus. Saul waited and waited without sight for THREE DAYS.

A believer named Ananias lived in Damascus. God told Ananias, "Go to Straight Street to help Saul." But Ananias knew Saul was cruel to believers. He was SCARED!

? ?
What do you do when you are scared?

"If you say so, I will go," said Ananias.

Ananias found Saul and laid his hands on him. "Jesus sent me to you so you could see and be filled with the Holy Spirit!" Ananias told Saul.

As soon as Ananias spoke, SCALES fell off of Saul's eyes! Saul could SEE!

Saul's life was CHANGED! Saul used to hurt believers. Now he told everyone, "JESUS really is the SON of God!"

Don't do it, Ananias! Saul's one of the bad guys.

There aren't "bad guys," Ruby. Jesus loves everyone.

Peter Raises Tabitha

ACTS 9:36-43

Peter was staying in Lydda, near Joppa. He healed people and shared the good news of Jesus. Two men from Joppa ran up to Peter. "Please come with us!" they cried. "Our friend Tabitha has died!"

Peter felt sad. Tabitha was a follower of Jesus. Her heart was BIG. She gave her time to sew tunics for people who needed clothes.

Everyone who knew Tabitha loved her. She was kind and helpful.

? ?
Who do you know who is kind and helpful?

Peter looked at the two men. Their eyes were filled with hope. "Take me to her house," he said.

Did you know Tabitha's name means gazelle?

Nope. Um, what's a gazelle?

Tabitha's home was filled with people. They cried out in sadness.

"God, why did you take Tabitha?"

"We miss her!"

"Who will make clothes for people in need?"

Peter stood beside Tabitha's body. A group of widows gathered around him. They cried and showed him the beautiful tunics Tabitha had sewn.

Peter asked them to leave so he could be alone. He knelt and prayed to God. Then he stood up and whispered in Tabitha's ear, "Tabitha, get up."

Tabitha's eyes popped open! She saw Peter and smiled. Peter held out his hand and helped her up.

When the widows saw Tabitha, they exclaimed, "Tabitha is ALIVE! It's a MIRACLE! God is SO good!"

Tabitha's story was told all over Joppa. More and more people believed in the Lord.

Now THAT is an amazing story! Peter raised someone from the dead. Jesus did that too!

I bet the widows are glad Tabitha can make clothes for people again.

Paul and Silas

ACTS 16:16-34

Paul and Silas were cold and hungry inside the dark stone prison.

They had freed a servant girl from a powerful spirit inside her. The girl's masters were angry. They BEAT Paul and Silas and THREW them in jail.

Paul and Silas were covered with cuts and bruises. Their bodies ached. But they trusted God was with them.

"God is good," they told the other prisoners. "Even when we are alone and cold and hurting, God is not far away. God is here."

Paul and Silas prayed and sang. "Glory to God! We are blessed!" The other prisoners listened and were comforted.

? ?

What songs help you feel better?

It's like I always say: Anything can be made better with a sing-along!

At midnight, a rumble shook the whole building. EARTHQUAKE!

The cell doors FLEW off their hinges!

The prison chains FELL from the prisoners' hands and feet!

"NO!" the jailer shouted. He was afraid. Had the prisoners run away? His masters would be furious!

"Hello?" whispered the jailer.

From inside the rubble, he heard Paul's voice.

"Don't be afraid!" Paul shouted. "We're all here!"

The jailer was AMAZED! Paul, Silas, and their friends trusted God to care for them. They didn't need to run.

That day, the jailer and his family were baptized. They were welcomed into God's family!

So the disciples sang so loud there was an earthquake? That rocks!

I think God had a lot to do with that earthquake, Otto. But it still rocks.

Roman Believers

ROMANS 4:13-25

Paul could hardly wait to visit Rome! He wanted to help the Roman believers learn more about God.

Rome was farther away from home than Paul had ever been before. He needed to sail across the sea to get there.

How long would it take him? More than one day, more than one week, more than one month, maybe even MORE than one whole YEAR!

Before Paul began his journey to Rome, he decided to write the people a letter. He knew God loved the Roman believers and they loved God. But he also thought they might have lots and lots of questions.

Paul asked God to help him know what to write.

I'd get seasick if I were on a boat for that long.

Maybe you could try writing a letter instead.

Dear Roman Believers,

   God gives us lots of rules. God's rules are important. But FAITH in God is MORE important than following rules all the time. Having faith means you trust God's promises, and God promises to love you, Jews and non-Jews, even when you make mistakes.

? ?
What mistakes have you made?

   Think of Abraham and Sarah's faith. God promised they would have a baby, even though they were very old. Abraham and Sarah had faith in God, and God gave them a baby!

   Jesus taught us to have faith that God ALWAYS loves us and forgives us. It's called grace! When you break a rule or make a mistake, God loves you. No matter what happens, have faith.

                                        Amen,
                                        Paul

So does following God's rules make God love us more?

It doesn't really work like that, Otto. God's love is the same no matter what we do.

Jews and Gentiles Together

ROMANS 15:4-13

The church in Rome included many different people.

SOME people were Jews.

SOME people were Gentiles.

EVERYONE believed in Jesus.

Paul wanted to encourage ALL of the believers.
He decided to send the people in the church a letter.

To the Church Family in Rome,

I heard you are arguing. Jews and Gentiles disagree about the best way to follow Jesus. I'm asking God to help you get along.

Paul sent a letter? Why, was everyone's phone turned off?

No, Ruby, because—

Relax, Leo, I was joking. I know they didn't have phones.

Don't live APART. Don't ARGUE. Live TOGETHER the way Jesus showed us!

You are ONE church. Worship God TOGETHER!

Welcome each other. Jesus welcomed EVERYONE!

? ?
How could you help someone feel welcome?

The scriptures were written to teach us. They give us hope that all God's people will live with God one day. The prophet Isaiah said Jesus is our hope.

Jews can have hope in Jesus.

Gentiles can have hope in Jesus.

EVERYONE can have hope in Jesus!

Jesus came, just like the scriptures said. I ask God to help EVERYONE believe in Jesus so you will have lots of hope TOGETHER!

> *Your friend,*
> *Paul*

Did it work? Did everyone do what Paul's letter said?

Probably. If he wrote it on really fancy paper.

One Body, Many Parts

1 CORINTHIANS 12:12-31a

The believers in Corinth were arguing. They thought SOME members of the church were MORE important than others. Paul knew ALL of God's people are important. Jews, Greeks, kids, and adults. ALL believers receive God's Spirit! He wrote the church in Corinth a letter.

Dear Friends in Corinth,

The church is like a body. We all have ONE body, but every body has MANY parts.

Each part of the body has its own job to do. There isn't one part that's better than the others.

? ?

What can you do with different parts of your body?

So even my toes have a job to do?

They help you walk, Otto.

374

Suppose the foot said, "I'm a foot. I'm not a hand. I can't do what the hand can do. I'm not part of the body!" That wouldn't be true!

What if the whole body was an eye? It would SEE very well, but how would it HEAR?

God made ONE body with MANY parts.

The church is the same way. We're all part of ONE church. And the church has MANY members. Pastors, choir members, teachers. Worship leaders, readers, and people who heal.

All the members have different gifts to share with the others. And we each need the gifts others bring too. If one member is hurting, we all hurt. If one member rejoices, we all rejoice.

Together we can love and care for each other, just like the parts of a body! Together we are the body of Christ.

Your friend,
Paul

Hey! I already knew that everyone is part of the body of Christ! Our pastor says that every week.

But this was the first time people heard this message, Otto.

God's Family

EPHESIANS 1:3-14

First, the apostles shared the sad news about Jesus' death. Then they shared the amazing good news of God raising Jesus from the dead. When people all over the world heard these stories, they started worshipping Jesus. The church was brand new!

Paul wrote a letter to people who started a new church in a city called Ephesus. He told them about how Jesus welcomes all of us into God's family.

Dear Ephesians,

Praise God! God has always been with us. Even before God made the world, God was thinking of you and me. God gives us a wonderful gift called GRACE. With God's grace, all our sins are forgiven. With God's grace, no matter what we do, we are loved!

It's hard to imagine the church as new. It's so old!

Even really, really old things were once new, like the furnace at our church.

378

How do we know about God's grace? Through Jesus! Jesus died and came back to life for YOU and ME. Because of Jesus, we KNOW God gives us grace. We KNOW God forgives us. We KNOW we are part of God's family.

Jesus taught us about God's promise—to bring EVERYONE together. To be ONE family. To LOVE and CARE for each other in the name of God.

? ?

Who is part of your church family?

Go and tell others about God's amazing gift. Go and bring new people into our family in Christ.

> *Your friend,*
> *Paul*

Anyone who wants to join is welcome in God's family!

Rejoice in the Lord

PHILIPPIANS 4:1-9

Paul loved traveling and teaching about Jesus. He helped early Christian believers create churches together. They wanted to share the good news of Jesus!

Some of the government leaders thought Paul was teaching people to dishonor the emperor by worshipping Jesus, so they threw him in prison.

Paul felt lonely in prison. "I miss my friends in Philippi," he thought. "I wonder how their church is doing. I know! I'll write them a letter!"

? ?

Who has written you a letter?

If I were in jail, I'd write letters all the time—mostly to help me get out of jail.

Dear Friends in Philippi,

I love you and miss you very much. Do you remember when Euodia, Syntyche, Clement, and I worked together to teach about Jesus? You wanted to learn even when it wasn't easy! Remind Euodia and Syntyche not to argue but to work together when they teach about Jesus!

REJOICE! Be happy! Don't worry about anything. Instead, pray about EVERYTHING! Pray like we prayed when we were together. Prayer will bring God into your hearts.

Remember what I said when I was with you. Think about what is true and fair. Praise God for everything. God is always with you!

Your friend,
Paul

Paul read through his letter again. He didn't feel lonely anymore. He found a way to keep sharing the good news with his friends!

Idea? Cinnamon? Clementine? Are they girl names? I'm not so sure.

You-OH-dee-uh and SIN-tih-chee were women in the church. KLEH-ment was a man.

Timothy's Report to Paul

I THESSALONIANS 3:9-13

Timothy kicked the dirt from his sandals and knocked on Paul's door. "Timothy, you're back!" Paul exclaimed when he saw his friend. Timothy had returned from a long trip visiting many new churches. The two men stepped inside.

? ?
What is the longest trip you have ever taken?

"How is the church in Thessalonica?" Paul asked.

"The church is growing!" Timothy replied. "Every day the Thessalonians tell more and more people about Jesus."

Paul smiled and clapped his hands. "That's good news!" he said.

"They still have lots of questions and wonder when they'll see you again. Maybe you could write them a letter," Timothy suggested.

Paul grabbed his stylus. "That sounds like a great idea!"

I can't imagine traveling back then. They only had feet, boats, and animals to get around.

Luckily, I'm a great rider! Do you want to see my stables?

Dear Thessalonians,

How can we thank God enough for you? You bring Timothy and me such joy!

We pray every night and day that we will see you again! It's a long trip to Thessalonica, but we hope to travel there again someday. Then we can answer your questions in person and restore your faith.

Timothy tells me the church is doing well—I am so pleased! Keep telling people about Jesus. Your church will continue to grow!

May God help you to love one another and all people. May your faith be strong until we meet again!

Grace and peace to you! AMEN!

Your friend in Christ,
Paul

Paul sure wrote a lot of letters.

Since he couldn't be everywhere, he let his letters do a lot of teaching.

Timothy's Faith

2 TIMOTHY 1:1-14

Paul felt lonely in prison. He thought about the trips he used to take with his good friend Timothy.

"Timothy is wonderful at teaching others about Jesus," thought Paul. "He was young when we first traveled together. Now he's a pastor! I wonder how he's doing."

Paul decided to write Timothy a letter.

Dear Timothy,

I love and miss you very much! You are in my prayers day and night. I wish we could see each other again!

I remember when we first met. You were very young, but you had a strong faith!

Your faith is a gift from God.

Your grandmother, Lois, had faith. Your mother, Eunice, had faith. Now, YOU have faith!

? ?

Who in your family has faith?

I wonder if Timothy's grandma Lois told the same stories about Jesus that my grandma tells me!

Remember to tell other people stories about God so their faith can grow too!

God was with us on our travels. God is with you in Ephesus, and God is with me in prison.

Tell people, "God is ALWAYS with us!"

Don't forget what we taught people when we were together. Jesus died and came back to life so that we can live with God FOREVER!

This is GOOD NEWS!

Everyone should hear it!

TELL them!

Remember, the Holy Spirit will help you.

Love,

Paul

Even though Paul was in prison, God was with him.

And even though Timothy wasn't in prison, God was with him too.

Taming the Tongue

JAMES 3:1-12

Some of the early believers were ARGUING.

"I don't want to share with you!"

"That's mine! Give it back!"

"You're not my friend!"

"Go away!"

One of Jesus' followers heard about these arguments. He wondered why many believers spoke such hurtful words. He decided to write a letter to the people in the early church.

Dear Friends,

Be careful what you say to each other. Your tongue is small. But your words can be LOUD. Don't be unkind. Don't tell lies. Small words can make a BIG difference.

When you ride a horse, you put a bit in its mouth. The bit is small, but it makes the horse go right. Or left. Or STOP! Your tongue is small. But it can be mean. Or kind. Or quiet.

I didn't know the Bible would have so much to say about my tongue. I thought it was just for tasting food.

You can use your tongue to say good things or bad things. Choose GOOD! Tell about Jesus' miracles! Share his teachings! Praise God!

Use kind words, not cruel ones. Talk about love, not hate.

? ?
What are kind words you can say every day?

If you are unkind, say, "I'm sorry!" Everyone makes mistakes. Everyone says the wrong thing sometimes. God forgives!

Your tongue is small, but it has a BIG job. Use your words to spread love and kindness to ALL God's people.

Signed,
A Follower of Jesus

Now if anyone says I talk too much, I'll tell them I have a small tongue with a BIG job.

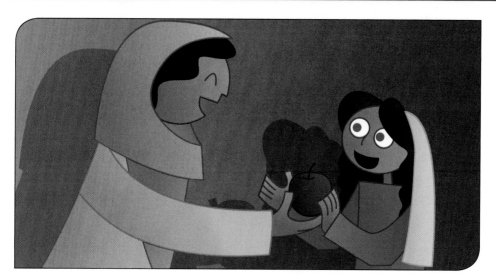

Alpha and Omega

REVELATION 1:4-8

ATTENTION, Churches in Asia!

John wrote a letter from his prison cell on an island called Patmos. He wanted Christians all over the world to know about God's faithfulness.

I'm sending you GRACE and PEACE from the all-powerful God! God is strong and will never leave you. God WAS! God IS! God will COME AGAIN!

? ?

What's something you look forward to happening again?

We know God because we know Jesus. Jesus taught us to love OTHERS the way God loves US. Jesus died for YOU and ME. Jesus came alive again. Never forget! The Messiah won against death.

 I wonder what John did to get thrown in prison.

 He probably got in trouble for spreading the news about Jesus. The emperor didn't want any competition.

ALL God's people are part of God's kingdom. If you live in the east or the west, YOU are in God's kingdom. If you live in the north or the south, YOU are in God's kingdom. No matter WHERE you live, YOU are in God's kingdom.

God is the ruler of EVERYTHING. Praise God forever! It's like the old song says:

"Look! Jesus comes, riding on a cloud!
Every eye will look and see,
Those who LOVE Jesus,
Those who HURT Jesus,
ALL will know he's here for you and me.

God is Alpha and Omega—
The beginning and the end.
God was, God is, God will come again,
Jesus, our savior and our friend!"

So God is the ruler of everything and everyone? Even little places like our town? Even you and me?

When John says everything, he means EVERYTHING.

New Heaven and New Earth

REVELATION 21:1-6

John of Patmos scribbled a letter as fast as he could. "Churches all over the world NEED to read about the visions God has sent me," he thought. "God told me to write about them!"

I MUST tell you ALL the things I've seen and heard!
God is always creating.
God is making something NEW out of something OLD.
God is making something GOOD out of something BAD.
God is creating RIGHT NOW.
A new HEAVEN! A new EARTH!

? ?
What do you like to create?

I KNOW it. I've SEEN it. I've HEARD it!
God has something WONDERFUL planned for us!

God's always making something new?

I like that. God's the ultimate inventor!

God SHOWED me the NEW world.

The old earth and heaven were GONE.
No more sea or land. No more trees or plants.

The holy city, Jerusalem, came down from heaven.
I heard a LOUD voice BOOM through the air.

> *"Look! See!*
> *God is WITH you!*
> *God will live with the people.*
> *Heaven and earth are ONE.*
> *No more sadness, only joy!*
> *No more death, only life!*
> *No more crying, only laughter!*
> *All the bad things in life are GONE forever.*
> *I am making ALL things NEW!"*

God is the Alpha and the Omega, the beginning and the end. God is EVERYTHING!

Remember this, children of God. No matter what, you are ALWAYS loved by God.

So the new world God's making will have even better things than this one.

That would be impressive. Because I've got some really nice stuff.

List of Stories and Scripture References

OLD TESTAMENT STORIES

Creation . . . . Genesis 1:1—2:4a

Adam and Eve . . . . Genesis 2:15-17; 3:1-7

Noah's Ark . . . . Genesis 6—9

Abraham and Sarah . . . . Genesis 15:1-12, 17-18;
17:1-7, 15-16

Sarah Laughs . . . . Genesis 18:1-15; 21:1-7

Isaac and Rebekah . . . . Genesis 24; 25:19-28

Jacob and Esau . . . . Genesis 27:1-40

Jacob Wrestles . . . . Genesis 32:22-31

Joseph and His Brothers . . . . Genesis 37:1-28

Joseph Interprets Dreams . . . . Genesis 39:20—41:57

Joseph Forgives His Brothers . . . . Genesis 45:3-11, 15

Baby Moses . . . . Exodus 2:1-10

The Burning Bush . . . . Exodus 3:1-15

The Ten Plagues . . . . Exodus 7:14—12:32

The Red Sea . . . . Exodus 14:1-30

Manna and Quail . . . . Exodus 16:1-35

The Ten Commandments . . . . Exodus 20:1-17

The Battle of Jericho . . . . Joshua 6:1-20

Deborah . . . . Judges 4—5

Ruth and Naomi . . . . Ruth 1

God Calls Samuel . . . . 1 Samuel 3:1-20

David Is Chosen . . . . 1 Samuel 16:1-13

David and Goliath . . . . 1 Samuel 17:1-49

Kings David and Solomon . . . . 2 Samuel 7:1-17;
1 Kings 2:10-12; 6

Elijah and Elisha . . . . 2 Kings 2:1-15

Queen Esther . . . . Esther 2:5-18; 3:1-6; 8:1-17

The Lord Is My Shepherd . . . . Psalm 23

Isaiah's Message . . . . Isaiah 2:1-5

God Calls Jeremiah . . . . Jeremiah 1:4-10

Daniel and the Lions . . . . Daniel 6

Jonah and the Big Fish . . . . Jonah 1; 2:1-2, 10; 3:1-5, 10

Malachi's Message . . . . Malachi 3:1-4

NEW TESTAMENT STORIES

The Annunciation . . . . Matthew 1:18-25;
Luke 1:26-38

Mary's Song . . . . Luke 1:39-55

Jesus Is Born . . . . Luke 2:1-20

Simeon and Anna . . . . Luke 2:22-40

The Wise Men . . . . Matthew 2:1-12

Escape to Egypt . . . . Matthew 2:13-23

Young Jesus in the Temple . . . . Luke 2:41-52

John the Baptist . . . . Mark 1:1-8

Jesus Is Baptized . . . . Luke 3:15-17, 21-22

Jesus Calls the Disciples . . . . Luke 5:1-11

The Beatitudes . . . . Matthew 5:1-12

Love Your Enemies . . . . Matthew 5:38-48

The Lord's Prayer . . . . Matthew 6:5-15

Don't Worry about Tomorrow . . . . Matthew 6:24-34

The Parable of the Sower . . . . Matthew 13:1-9, 18-23

Jesus Walks on Water . . . . Matthew 14:22-33

Jesus Teaches about Forgiveness . . . . Matthew 18:21-35

The Parable of the Vineyard . . . . Matthew 20:1-16

Jesus and the Pharisees . . . . Matthew 22:15-22

The Greatest Commandment . . . . Matthew 22:34-40

Serving People, Serving Jesus . . . . Matthew 25:31-46

Healing at Simon's House . . . . Mark 1:29-39

A Man through a Roof . . . . Mark 2:1-12

Jesus Calms the Storm . . . . Mark 4:35-41

Who's the Greatest? . . . . Mark 9:30-37

Jesus Blesses the Children . . . . Mark 10:13-16

A Camel through a Needle . . . . Mark 10:17-31

Bartimaeus Sees . . . . Mark 10:46-52

The Widow's Offering . . . . Mark 12:41-44

The Transfiguration . . . . Luke 9:28-36

The Good Samaritan . . . . Luke 10:25-37

Mary and Martha . . . . Luke 10:38-42

The Lost Sheep and Lost Coin . . . . Luke 15:1-10

The Prodigal Son . . . . Luke 15:11-32

Jesus Heals Ten . . . . Luke 17:11-19

Zacchaeus . . . . Luke 19:1-10

Water into Wine . . . . John 2:1-11

Nicodemus . . . . John 3:1-17

The Woman at the Well . . . . John 4:5-30

Jesus Feeds 5,000 . . . . John 6:1-21

The Good Shepherd . . . . John 10:11-18

Jesus Raises Lazarus . . . . John 11:1-45

Mary Anoints Jesus . . . . John 12:1-8

Jesus the Vine . . . . John 15:1-17

Jesus Enters Jerusalem........................ Matthew 21:1-11;
                                             Luke 19:28-40

The Last Supper .... Matthew 26:14-29;
                                             Luke 22:14-23

Jesus Is Betrayed .... Mark 14:26-50

Jesus Is Crucified .... Luke 23:26-56

Jesus Is Risen .... Matthew 28:1-10;
                                             John 20:1-18

On the Road to Emmaus..................... Luke 24:13-35

Thomas Wonders............................. John 20:19-31

The Great Commission .... Matthew 28:16-20

Jesus Ascends .... Acts 1:6-14

The Holy Spirit at Pentecost............... Acts 2:1-21

Early Believers Share........................ Acts 4:32-35

Saul's Conversion .... Acts 9:1-20

Peter Raises Tabitha .... Acts 9:36-43

Paul and Silas................................ Acts 16:16-34

Roman Believers .... Romans 4:13-25

Jews and Gentiles Together .... Romans 15:4-13

One Body, Many Parts....................... 1 Corinthians 12:12-31a

God's Family .... Ephesians 1:3-14

Rejoice in the Lord .... Philippians 4:1-9

Timothy's Report to Paul .... I Thessalonians 3:9-13

Timothy's Faith.............................. 2 Timothy 1:1-14

Taming the Tongue.......................... James 3:1-12

Alpha and Omega .... Revelation 1:4-8

New Heaven and New Earth .... Revelation 21:1-6